More Than Tongues Can Tell

D1610802

By the same authors

Spiritual Gifts and the Church   (Inter-Varsity Press)
The Water that Divides   (Inter-Varsity Press)
The Meal that Unites   (Hodder & Stoughton)

By Donald Bridge

God has Resources   (Paternoster)

More Than Tongues Can Tell

Reflections on Charismatic Renewal
Donald Bridge and David Phypers

Foreword by David Watson

HODDER AND STOUGHTON
LONDON SYDNEY AUCKLAND TORONTO

British Library Cataloguing in Publication Data

Bridge, Donald
  More than tongues can tell.
  1. Spiritual life
  I. Title   II. Phypers, David
  269   BV4501.2

ISBN 0 340 32018 4

FOREWORD

It has always been an important practice of Christ's disciples to encourage faith by sharing with one another the mighty acts of God. 'They gathered the church together and declared all that God had done with them' (Acts 14:27); 'They listened to Barnabas and Saul as they related what signs and wonders God had done through them' (Acts 15:12); 'He related one by one the things that God had done . . . through his ministry' (Acts 21:19). In our materialistic society it is all too easy to be earthbound, unbelieving, even cynical. We forget that God is God. We doubt that the God of the New Testament is still the God of today. We reduce him to the level of our small minds, and wonder why most people respond, "But that I can't believe!"

Unquestionably, God is doing something new by his Spirit throughout the world today. Some of it is obscured by inevitable excesses and abuses, or else confused by bad theology. 'Charismatic renewal' is good news for some, bad news for others. Nevertheless, in our bleak and dangerous world the need to stimulate faith in the living God is immense. The early Christians turned their world upside down simply because they dared to believe in God with whom *all* things are possible. As a result, the lame walked, the blind saw, demons were cast out, and vast numbers believed. Today's prevailing apathy would not have been possible. God was manifestly amongst them.

I am so grateful to Donald Bridge and David Phypers for what is essentially a faithbuilding book. With honesty they have recorded what God has done through their ministry and church, especially during their years in Sunderland. They have written about God's power to heal, and yet have shared their puzzlement at times in the whole area of healing; this book is not just another triumphalist success story. They have been open about their original fears and misgivings concerning charismatic renewal. They have shown how their prejudiced Protestant evangelical attitudes towards Roman Catholics have been significantly changed. Yet, throughout, they have revealed a right concern for biblical Christianity and for spiritual renewal within the historic Churches.

This is a story of God's actions by God's Spirit to the glory of God's Son. The fastmoving narrative is, however, shot through with sound biblical insights, wise pastoral instruction and clear spiritual vision. The assessment of renewal, in the final chapter, is one of the best that I have seen: fair, searching, challenging.

Any openminded reader will find in this book much to encourage faith in the God whose thoughts and ways are so much bigger and better than our own.

David Watson

CONTENTS

PREFACE

Ten years have passed since we first ventured into print with *Spiritual Gifts and the Church*. Conservative evangelicals, deeply hesitant about Pentecostalism, we had been forced to reassess our position by the process of renewal we had jointly experienced. The story of that renewal can now be told.

All the events recorded in this book are true. Most of them occurred between 1966 and 1972 when we were pastor and deacon respectively at Enon Baptist Church in Sunderland. Some have been added from later years. To preserve anonymity, names of those involved and some incidental details have been changed.

Writing about ourselves has not been easy. John the Baptist said of Jesus and himself, "He must increase, but I must decrease" (John 3:30). That, we hope, has been our attitude as well. At another level we have had the problem of conveying our separate and combined involvement in the events we have recorded. So what follows is a grateful account of God's dealings with two very ordinary and imperfect people during a formative period of their lives. What happened was God's way with us. It will almost certainly not be his exact way with anyone else, for God is a loving Father who treats his children according to their own particular needs. In the text 'Don' and 'David' refer to ourselves. 'We' denotes our combined involvement and opinion. Our particular thanks go to Rosalind Doig for proof-reading the text and for suggesting the title, *More Than Tongues Can Tell*.

The renewal of the church has barely begun. In parts of the United Kingdom at least, it seems already to be running out of steam. It is our hope and prayer that, through this sequel to *Spiritual Gifts and the Church*, God will rekindle love that has grown cold, and ignite with the fire of his Holy Spirit those who have never known his renewing, life-giving power.

Frinton-on-Sea, Essex
Derby, England 1982

CHAPTER 1 – NEW BEGINNINGS

"Remember, whatever happens, never give up! Keep cool. Concentrate. You're the best in the world. We're going to win!" Beneath the towering stands of Wembley Stadium, Alf Ramsay was giving his last quiet briefing to the star-studded England football squad. The sporting spectacle of the twentieth century, the 1966 World Cup Final against West Germany, was about to begin. Packed on the terraces above, a hundred thousand delirious fans waved flags, banners and scarves, chanting incessantly, 'England! England!' Outside, thousands more milled excitedly about, vainly trying to obtain any last few tickets which would magically admit them to a coveted place in the mighty arena. Further afield, millions of men, women and children sat expectantly around their television sets, waiting for the game to start. The future of the world, it seemed, hung on the efforts of twenty-two men kicking a piece of inflated leather around the hallowed Wembley turf during the next ninety minutes.

"And so I know God's richest blessing will rest on David and Margaret in their married life together. We wish them every happiness and great joy . . ." David's father was saying a last few public words to his son and daughter-in-law at their wedding reception. But the guests were already shifting uneasily in their seats. For the hands of the clock had crept past three. The wedding, delightful as it had been, was over. Minds were now set on more serious things: a retreat to the bar where the television set was receiving the game from Wembley. Ever since they had realised that they had planned to marry on World Cup day, David and Margaret had known that the wedding and football would have to co-exist. It all fitted rather well, really. The reception formalities could end by three. The match would finish at twenty to five. A train left from the local station half an hour later, giving the guests ample time to stretch their legs and wave the newly-weds a last good-bye. How convenient! But after losing an early lead, West Germany equalised in the eighty-ninth minute. The game went into extra time, and the happy couple left for wedded bliss from an almost deserted railway platform.

Two weeks of Majorcan sun later, David and Margaret were letting themselves into their new home in Sunderland on the north-east coast of England. David had taken a post as Head of Religious Education in one of the town's high schools; Margaret was looking forward to teaching in a grammar school. Three more weeks of holiday remained before work began, precious days of adjustment to the exciting demands of married life.

Both David and Margaret had enjoyed a Christian up-bringing. Ever since he could remember, David had been taken, every Sunday and often on weekdays, to a tiny, independent mission church in the heart of Sheffield, York-shire. When he was nine, and again at seventeen, he had enjoyed personal experiences of Jesus Christ as Saviour and Lord. Margaret had attended her local Church of England Sunday School throughout her childhood and had been duly confirmed when she was fourteen. Personal faith had followed two years later through the instruction of a dedicated teacher of Religious Education and the witness of the school Christian Union.

Now they were starting a new life together a hundred and twenty miles from home. Waiting on the doormat on their return from honeymoon was a letter from Donald Bridge, welcoming them to the town and to worship and fellowship at Enon Baptist Church where he had recently become the minister.

Sunderland lies only eleven miles south-east of New-castle, and there is scarcely any open country between the town and the city. To the uninitiated, a move from one to the other seems to offer no change at all. In actual fact, the psychological shift is quite drastic. Men of Sunderland are not 'Geordies', and they are irritated to be labelled as such by ignorant southerners – that is, people living south of the River Tees. The sing-song voice and thickened word-endings of Newcastle are replaced by a more dour tone and by the flat vowels of Wearside. The emotionalism of Tyne-side has given away to the phlegm of County Durham. Old traditions die hard, and new ideas are treated with cautious suspicion. In the seventh century a party of Christian monks, eager to evangelise the Anglo-Saxons of Wearside, were swept out to sea as they attempted to cross the river by raft. To their horror, the local boatmen watched stolidly from the bank without offering help. One gave voice to the feelings of them all: "They have taken our old ways from us, and what they bring us we do not know. Let them save themselves." Sunderland today still takes a lot of persuading to change its mind.

In spite of that, the town has a great Christian tradition. The monks kept on coming, and in 673 the monastery of St. Peter defiantly raised its grey stone walls on the windswept cliff-tops above the mouth of the Wear. Here in his child-hood the gentle and pious Bede heard the call of God. Here, and at nearby Jarrow, he laid the foundations of modern historical knowledge with his monumental *Ecclesiastical History of the English People*, still widely read in paperback thirteen centuries later. Here he wrote the first-ever Anglo-Saxon Bible commentaries, eagerly sought-after to the boundaries of Christendom. Here, most of all, he had his vision of a Bible translated into English. Here, his last words were a whispered translation of the closing sentences of John's Gospel.

The monks at the mouth of the Wear gave the name Monkwearmouth to the north bank of the river. The Anglo-Saxon settlement which grew on the south bank found ready work and wages for its men as the schemes of the evangelists demanded more and more buildings, but the cautious labourers crossed back in their boats to the safe paganism of the sundered-land each night. Monkwear-mouth and Sunderland are now one town, linked by three great bridges, but the north side is still jokingly called 'the Christian side'.

11

Ancient St Peter's Church still stands, no longer a monastery but a parish church of the Church of England. A shipyard surrounds it on three sides. A mighty crane dwarfs its once-defiant tower. In the technological revolution of the mid-sixties the sanctuary was filled every weekday with the sounds of heavy industry, the roar of machines, the clatter of trucks, the staccato stammer of riveting. The sounds and the skyline proclaimed a parable – around the River Wear the hard fight for material gain had eclipsed most spiritual values. Thousands poured into the shipyard. Only a handful worshipped in the church.

Two hundred yards away, the local Baptists found it hard work, too, and it was to give leadership to them that Don had come to Sunderland just three months before the World Cup Final and David's and Margaret's wedding. Born and reared in a Plymouth Brethren home in nearby Stockton-on-Tees, he had imbibed that exhaustive knowledge of the Bible which is one of the hallmarks of the movement. When he was twenty three an evangelist with the Open Air Mission had been struck dead by lightning at Ascot racecourse, and Don had responded to God's call to fill the gap left by his death. Seven years of travelling preaching had followed. Speakers' Corner in Hyde Park, Liverpool Pier Head, Nottingham Town Hall Square, every racecourse in the land, indoor missions when invited by churches of every kind – anywhere and everywhere where folk would listen, Don and a colleage preached the gospel of the grace of God in Christ in simple terms that all could understand. And the seed sown bore fruit. Most passed on, some scoffed, others reacted angrily and violently, but week by week some trusted Christ for forgiveness and new life.

The experience became, for Don, a more effective training for the ministry than he could ever have received in a theological college. For a start, it taught him to hold and keep his audience. If his open-air preaching was boring he simply lost his crowd, if he had ever gained it in the first place. So he learned the art of contemporary story and illustration in the presentation of the good news. Also, and quite unconsciously, he discovered the value of visual attraction. His bent nose gave him a humorous appearance, while his pensive, wistful face lit up before an important point was made. In the open air he learned to express theological truth without theological jargon, and to relate that truth to the problems and fears of the common man. He also came to appreciate and to work with Christians of every kind. The open air broadened Don in every way, and delivered him from some of the narrower, inhibiting attitudes on secondary issues which so often keep Brethren apart from their fellow-believers.

In time, Don became frustrated with simple evangelism. He longed to nurture those he won for Christ, rather than pass them on to someone else. So for four years he pastored a Free Church in Newcastle before being ordained into the Baptist ministry and welcomed to the leadership of the Enon Church in Sunderland.

Methodism is the great nonconformist religion of County Durham, and Baptists are thin on the ground. On the south side of the river a chapel to seat seven hundred was the centre for twenty demoralised worshippers. On the north side, the compulsory demolition of an almost equally large building to open the way for slum clearance and redevelopment had put funds into the hands of a further forty-five members to build a splendid new church. Designed to seat a modest hundred and fifty, with adjoining hall, modern kitchen and other rooms forming a neat square, the whole complex was crowned with a simple wooden cross, proclaiming that the shipyard crane was not to have things all its own way.

Monkwearmouth was to be Don's area, but no secret was made of the hope that he would persaude the twenty fellow-Baptists on the south side to close their beloved chapel and join in forming one solid base for future work. Don's plans for that future were based on lessons, positive and negative, learned in hectic years pastoring the Free Church in nearby Newcastle.

First, there must be regular, systematic teaching of the Bible, aimed to give a knowledge of its contents and an application of its challenge: this might be described as *popular exposition*. Then, there must be a pressing home of the claims of Christ in the gospel, done in such a way that the right to preach was won by the demonstration of a practical caring for people: *pastoral evangelism*, that could be called. Lastly, there must be opportunity for people to worship God with enthusiasm and vigour, expressing themselves in meaningful ways, drawing on the riches of all Christian traditions, and finding new ways of their own: that could be thought of as *contemporary worship*. Conversions were only likely to occur when a nucleus of Christians understood their faith and enthused about it enough to share it with others.

Enon's parish was very restricted, bounded by sea to the east, river and shipyard to the south, busy main road to the west, shopping-centre to the north. Within it was a mixture of drab, newly-built flats already beginning to look like prison blocks, and older street-houses built back-to-back in soot-encrusted rows. In a radius of a quarter of a mile the scarcely-felt spiritual needs of the local working-class folk were served by Anglicans, Roman Catholics, Methodists, Pentecostals, Baptists, an independent mission and the Salvation Army. Any genuinely local impact was largely restricted to gaining Sunday-school children at each other's expense. The adults were almost untouched, glancing occasionally at the churches over a yawning chasm of entirely artificial class distinction.

In actual fact, church-goers and non-churchgoers were basically of the same class and earned the same amounts of money. What created the gap was the way they spent it. Christians were more thrifty, more disciplined, and found no attraction in the public-houses, bingo halls and betting-shops which sprouted at every street corner during the prosperous nineteen-sixties. The result was that they could afford to buy houses instead of renting them. But the whole area offered only rented property. So the Christian house-owners began to live a mile away. Faithful to their old churches, they came in by motor-car to worship. Those cars standing outside the church doors became an odd symbol of sociological barrier. The local flat-dwellers expressed near hatred for them and their drivers. They were believed to symbolise abounding wealth, social injustice and arrogant snobbery. In vain did Don try to point out that with the money they spent on tobacco, beer and betting, flat-dwellers could quite easily buy cars of their own, or, for that matter, houses of their own. There stood the vehicles outside the church doors, golden chariots whose shining surfaces hinted at dishonest gain and exploitation of the masses. Christianity was for car-drivers, not ordinary, honest working men. "Perhaps," Don thought, "I should ask the members of my congregation to join in a great act of self-renunciation, and walk to church . . ."

Enon, however, was not yet strong enough to tackle the prejudices of this restricted area. Until it was, and indeed to help it so to become, it must draw on a wider constituency in order to build up its numbers and resources. It must become a preaching church, a centre to which any who had a desire for truth and certainty might come. The popular exposition must be given priority. Meanwhile, what channels there were would be kept open to the flat-dwelling neighbours. Children's work could be developed. Christian newspapers with a *Daily Mirror* format could be distributed monthly. Every birth, marriage, illness, accident and death could be followed up by a visitation team offering friendship and a listening ear.

Don found immediate encouragement. A series of Sunday morning expositions on Peter's First Letter reminded church members of the great foundations of their faith and its practical implications. Evening sermons on the Apostles' Creed, entitled 'A Faith for the Nineteen-Sixties', answered modern objections and offered age-old solutions to current problems. Students, with and without faith, from the Technical College and the College of Education, began to attend in good numbers. David and Margaret, attracted by a quality of preaching they had rarely heard since their own student days, quickly became enthusiastic members of the small but growing worshipping community. Strangers in a strange town whose local lingo could be as mystifying as a foreign language, they were welcomed, not only to the meetings and activities at the church, but into the homes of many of the members. Other zealous Christians coming to reside in Sunderland at about the same time also joined the church and offered their help.

Members found it was possible to bring the occasional friend and relative to church, and then to see them wanting to come back again. Numbers attending services steadily rose. The little weekly prayer-meeting expanded and had to move out of a side-room into the hall. Best of all, a visible impact was made on the lives of some who began to attend. The very first housewife Don visited admitted to being a 'lapsed Presbyterian' and began to join the congregation. Dying embers of childhood faith were stirred into life. She left carefully-chosen books around the house for her atheistic husband to read. Glancing through one of them, he came across the words of Jesus, "You will not come to me" (John 5:40). Shaking with emotion, he wrote out a list of his past misdeeds, set it on fire, and came to ask for Christian baptism. When he, his wife and nine others were baptised six months later, every seat in the modest church was filled, the aisles were blocked, and the doors were opened for people standing in the porch to watch. Older members spoke of being more sure of their faith than ever before. New converts brought contacts with fresh circles of relatives and friends who might be reached for Christ. In a far shorter time than Don had originally anticipated, popular exposition was leading to pastoral evangelism, and the church building was regularly full.

'Success' in the Christian ministry is hard to define and harder still to analyse. Spiritual values cannot be measured in any of the terms familiar to secular man. Clearly, numbers are no criterion at all. Some of the most tragic apostates in the Protestant pulpit have attracted large congregations and built up impressive organisations. Faithfulness to one's commission is a safer guide. "Be instant in season and out. Do the work of an evangelist" (2 Tim 4:5). When that is done, the consequences will vary from place to place. St Paul was despised in Corinth and took Ephesus by storm.

Richard Baxter set nearly every family in seventeenth-century Kidderminster praying: a contemporary, equally faithful, preached the same doctrines and saw two conversions during his whole ministry. Nevertheless, Christian service, and especially Christian preaching, should be seen to be effective in some way. The first two years in Sunderland strengthened that conviction in a hundred ways.

CHAPTER 2 – NEW DEMANDS

"Brrr, brrr! Brrr, brrr! Brrr, brrr . . ." The bedside tele-phone screamed a dozen times before Don groped sleepily for the receiver. "We need you, Don! Come quickly!" a woman sobbed, at the end of the line. Recognising the voice at once, Don scrambled out of bed, hastily pulling trousers and a sweater on top of his pyjamas. An October moon silvered the cobbled lane as he pushed the car out of the garage, anxious not to disturb sleeping neighbours. Soon he was speeding through open country towards the Tyne.

Half an hour later Don was ushered into a house whose every window was alight. A grim-faced father was ransack-ing every room, pulling out drawers and emptying them, feeling behind cushions, mounting a chair to examine the tops of cupboards and wardrobes. A pallid mother gripped Don's arm and began to weep. A young man lay on a couch, yellow-faced, hair damp with perspiration, mouth twisted with pain. His shirt gaped open, and his chest was bleeding as he tore at it with his finger-nails.

Don's heart faltered as he took in the scene: withdrawal symptoms from drug addiction. He had read all about them. Like thousands of other Christians at that time, he knew scenes from David Wilkerson's *The Cross and the Switchblade* by heart. All were aware of British leaders warning that 'it could happen here', and that a permissive-minded government was as uninterested as it was in warn-ings about alcoholism, organised gambling and wholesale abortions. It *could* happen here. It was happening, now, before Don's very eyes.

Young Kenneth had slid imperceptibly down the slippery slope soon to be so familiar to bewildered parents and teachers. First of all the occasional 'pep pill' to stimulate him for a late-night dance. Then the so-called 'soft' drugs in increasing quantity. Then the stage where it was no longer much fun to take them, but to be without them meant uneasiness and restlessness. Then the really fatal step as the 'hard' drugs were taken, and heroin began its deadly, nightmare work.

Now he wanted to get off drugs, and had gone 'cold turkey', cutting off the supply immediately and completely without the aid of milder drugs. One of the less unpleasant effects of this is that the skin goose-pimples to resemble that of a plucked fowl. At that moment, a queer skin was the least of Kenneth's problems. He faced at least a week of living hell and further weeks of milder discomfort, innocuously called 'withdrawal symptoms' before his body adjusted again to life without drugs.

How on earth could Don help? Another spasm contorted Kenneth's face and body as Don knelt beside the couch. Pulling out his pocket Bible, he read aloud the old familiar words of the fortieth psalm:

> I waited patiently for the LORD;
> he inclined to me and heard my cry.
> He drew me up from the desolate pit,
>   out of the miry bog,
> and set my feet upon a rock,
>   making my steps secure (verses 1,2).

Kenneth's bloodshot eyes fixed Don with a despairing gaze, and his grip hurt Don's wrist. What now? Often when Don had prayed with people after they had shared great problems, he had felt the urge to go a bit further. Yes, they had asked God to do something, but why not do it now, immediately? Were prayer and faith a mere pious formula, an expression of hope but not of expectation? More than once in such circumstances, Don's hand had almost itched to be laid on the head of the sufferer, as an expression of a burning conviction that God could intervene there and then. This time he did not restrain the instinct. He placed his hands on Kenneth's head. There was nothing else he could do. "Kenneth, in the name of Jesus, be at peace." Kenneth's eyes closed, and he fell peacefully asleep. Don drew a deep, trembling breath, and put his hands firmly in his pockets! It was his first charismatic experience, and he hardly knew what to make of it.

Someone has said that your opinion of the charismatic movement is like your opinion of the Lord Mayor's Show: it depends on whether you are taking part in it, watching it, or clearing up the mess left behind it! In fact, the classification is not quite so simple nor so mutually exclusive as that. Many Christians have found themselves in all three roles at different times. Sometimes they are even in all three at once.

We had both known Pentecostals of the old type ever since our teens. In fact the British Pentecostal movement had started just round the corner from Enon in the parish church of All Saints, Monkwearmouth. There, in the early years of the twentieth century, the vicar, Canon Alexander Boddy, and many members of the congregation, had been filled with the Spirit and had spoken in tongues. As we walked to and from Enon along the Fulwell Road, we often wondered at a strange inscription on one of the foundation stones of the parish church hall:

September 1907
WHEN
THE FIRE OF THE LORD
FELL
IT BURNED UP THE DEBT.

Whatever was that all about?

For several reasons British Pentecostalism had failed to realise its early potential. Quickly splitting from the 'main-line' churches which had given it birth, it had split again into three main groups and a host of smaller ones. By the nineteen-fifties, Pentecostals were still a tiny minority among British Christians as a whole. Scorned for their 'sheep-stealing' whereby they built up their congregations at the expense of others, suspected for their reported scenes of emotionalism, excess and extravagant claims, they were largely spurned by their fellow-Christians in the older, larger churches. Few were aware of their astonishing growth in Latin America and of their impact on the emerging societies of that distant continent.

The late fifties, however, brought a new awareness of this type of Christianity. Strange stories began to circulate of a new Pentecostalism now sweeping the 'main-line' Protestant churches again. As long as the stories came only from California, that home of most things weird and wonderful, no one took a great deal of notice. But by the mid-sixties the issues raised were becoming a major pastoral problem in Britain. Any minister was liable to find a church-member on his doorstep claiming to have been baptised in the Spirit. Midweek prayer-meetings ran the hazard of an enthusiast speaking in tongues. Ministers' fraternals, normally devoted to placid plans for Christian Aid Week, found themselves forced to discuss prophecy and miraculous healing.

To complicate things further, startling news emerged that the movement had spilled over into the Roman Catholic Church. There, its consequences appeared to verge on the schizophrenic, making its adherents talk like evangelicals, pray like Pentecostals, and behave like Jesuits. What on earth was happening?

The aggressive nature of our evangelism in Sunderland made it inevitable that the issue would arise. We not only believed the Gospel, but we also expected it to work, and positively thrust it before the attention of all kinds of people. Some of these came from utterly irreligious backgrounds. Others' domestic affairs were in the most appalling mess. Yet others, finding contemporary materialism an arid and thirsty desert, had dabbled in the occult.

The perfectly normal Christian approach to all such people was to help them to an awareness of what God has to say in the Bible about their situation. Part of that biblical message is the need for a vital spiritual experience, a personal encounter with Jesus Christ. Another part is the insistence that God can be proved to be a living reality in everyday life. He provides guidance in perplexity, inner

21

strength for those under pressure, and everything necessary for a life consistent with Christian allegiance.

Not surprisingly, some pretty startling problems began to be dropped into the laps of our church leaders. Richard and Brenda, for example, became deeply involved in personal counselling amoung students. Approaching middle age at that time, they both had solid Christian backgrounds. Richard, six feet tall, broad-shouldered, and with a liking for tweedy jackets, was a local college lecturer. His mild nature was expressed in a placid round face, unfashionably short hair, and the slightly oriental eyes of someone who has just given up spectacles for contact lenses. Brenda, equally professional, was the broad-faced motherly type to whom people found themselves attracted whenever they were in trouble. Just a shade tougher and more practical than Richard, she had a shrewd common sense that expressed itself in flat northern vowels . . . and a fund of warm good-heartedness.

Brenda needed her common sense and Richard his patience when dealing with the problems which came their way. Inviting students to tea and then on to church to hear some of Don's provocative sermons, they soon found themselves confronted with drug-addiction, depression, obsessive habits and emotional disorders. Naturally enough, they sometimes found themselves at a loss.

One night they discussed their situation with Don. Together, they ran over the obvious points: the need to avoid being judgmental, the pointlessness of being shocked, the value of listening, the importance of reaching the real emotional and spiritual root of a problem. Suddenly, Richard leaned forward, wrapping his arms round one of his knees. He seemed rather nervous.

"Don, is there not some further spiritual experience, some tapping of spiritual power, that would better equip us to help people like these?"

"Not that I know of," replied Don. "Be grateful for the successes and don't take the failures too much to heart. God has his own way of working, and as often as not you will be just one link in a chain of circumstances."

"All right. Yes. Grand." Brenda's dialect always broadened on the rare occasions when she became excited. "But can't we expect a bit more than lofty hopes that sometime, somewhere your chain of circumstances will have a happy end? We are talking about kids who need saving *now*. Answers the day after tomorrow are too late."

"What about the Holy Spirit?" interposed Richard quietly.

"Well, the Holy Spirit is the spiritual presence of Christ within you. That's precisely what makes you a Christian in the first place."

"And what about being filled with the Holy Spirit?" Richard pressed, even more quietly, with a gentle blinking of his mild eyes.

Don sighed. "All right, the two of you! Out with it! You've been flirting with the Pentecostals, haven't you?"

The flirtation had, in fact, been very minor. The Easter Convention at the local Elim church had attracted their curiosity. After one of the meetings they had learned in casual conversation that a local Baptist minister just north of the Tyne had been 'filled with the Holy Spirit', with impressive results.

Don sighed again. "Look, I can only go by what the Bible says. I'd like to believe there is some great experience which turns us into spiritual supermen. But I just can't find it in the Bible. Read Christ's teaching about the Holy Spirit. Study St Paul's great doctrinal letters. They don't mention anything about two classes of Christians. Sure, an account sometimes says, 'He was filled with the Holy Spirit.' That is a comment by the author, or by spectators. You never find anyone saying, 'I am filled with the Holy Spirit.' The expression describes a quality of life, not a dramatic experience."

"Then what about the disciples on the day of Pentecost, and the Samaritans when Peter laid his hands on them? Weren't those dramatic experiences?" Richard and Brenda were not satisfied.

"Yes, certainly, but look at all the incidents in the Acts of the Apostles, and you'll have an awful job to find a uniform pattern. 'Baptised', 'filled', 'poured out', 'anointed', 'falling upon them' – a dozen different expressions are used. Didn't Jesus warn us that the Spirit is as free and unpredictable as the wind? I honestly do not see any fixed pattern for finding more spiritual power, and I am uneasy about any suggestion that the work of Christ in a believer's life is in some way incomplete and needs to be supplemented. My advice to you is to go ahead when chances come to help people, and simply to guard your personal lives from the kind of things you know grieve God. Then believe that he will use you."

Richard and Brenda remained unconvinced. They were good enough friends to tell Don so without hard feelings on either side. So he was not at all surprised when they courteously told him they were going to consult another minister. Nor was he surprised when they returned to describe how the minister had laid his hands on their heads and prayed with them. Nothing spectacular had happened at the time. Both simply had a feeling of elation and relief. But later, praying at home, first Richard and then Brenda had discovered the ability to pray in unknown words. Convinced that God would use and equip them in new and powerful ways, they soon found needy folk beating a path to their door even more frequently than before. Eager to share their experience with others, they opened their home for monthly meetings of prayer and praise where spiritual gifts could be exercised, the fullness of the Spirit received, and victory claimed in the name of Jesus for any who were troubled and distressed.

Jim, a research student at the college, became one of the first to share Richard's and Brenda's new experience. Ironically, he had come to Sunderland from Elim Pentecostals in Lancashire, where their strict black-or-white distinctions and inward-looking pietism had failed to catch his enthusiasm. Almost the double of *University Challenge*'s Bamber Gascoigne, he possessed great sensitivity.

"You've done the trick since I came to Sunderland," he assured Don. "Your vivid word-pictures from the Bible, your convincing and satisfying Calvinistic theology, your promotion of the big view are just what I've needed. So what happens?" He took off his spectacles and polished them absentmindedly. "Good theology makes me want very much to be a better Christian. Great teaching about the sovereignty of God makes me long to please him. So I spend much more time in prayer with all the seriousness of which I'm capable. I give myself to him. Then what happens?" He leaned back and ran his hand through his hair. "The next thing I know, I'm filled with elation and start speaking in tongues. The folk back home would say I've been baptised with the Holy Spirit. And the very next thing that happens, I'm elected by popular vote as president of the Students' Union. That brings a lot of influence, I can tell you. But I feel able to tackle it with this new energy God has given me."

Whatever Don might have thought about Pentecostal teaching, the reality of what was happening could not be gainsaid. Perhaps it was time to think again.

CHAPTER 3 – NEW RESOURCES

White, fluffy clouds drifted lazily across a bright, clear sky. Seals basked and mewed on the rocks. Gulls cried and whirled above a sparkling sea. Shags, cormorants and kittiwakes clung to inaccessible ledges on towering cliffs beneath the gaunt ruins of Dunstanburgh Castle. Don was in retreat, alone in a solitary log-cabin on the Northumberland coast, pondering and praying over the dramatic events of recent months.

He had much with which to occupy his mind. Reared and converted in a thoroughly evangelical tradition, he was instinctively repelled by anything which smacked remotely of 'second-blessing' theology. "You cannot add anything to the work of Christ." That was his first and last conviction. He did not need to turn to any biblical passage to prove it, for he knew them all by heart. He murmured one aloud as he walked along the empty beach: "God . . . has blessed us in Christ with *every* spiritual blessing" (Ephesians 1:3).

That was the whole basis of Don's preaching and his personal faith. Beyond the golden sands and splashing waves, faces filled his mind, faces of people from all walks of life whom he had persuaded to take in faith the hand of Christ. Had he, after all, offered them less than a complete gospel? Perish the thought! His ingrained knowledge of God's word insisted that that could never be the case. What, then, of Richard and Brenda and the scholarly Jim, who claimed that his ministry had led them to ask for more, and to find it? More of what?

Don stopped and stared out across the restless sea. "The baptism of the Spirit," they were calling it. Richard had smiled apologetically when he had first used the phrase, murmuring, "I'm not much bothered about words and names. The experience is the thing, and that phrase seems

26

to cover it as well as any. Immersed in the Spirit – a fair Baptist term, I should have thought."

Jim had been even less insistent. "My folk back home call it the baptism, and it seems biblical enough," he had grinned, polishing his spectacles and blinking up half-nervously. "But I'm not going to fall out about it. 'Fullness.' 'Anointing'. Call it what you like."

Again, Don felt troubled. A second experience 'of the Spirit'? But "anyone who does not have the Spirit of Christ does not belong to him" (Romans 8:9). How could anyone be a Christian and not have the Spirit? Was not this the point of Jesus's words to Nicodemus? To enter the kingdom of God he had to be born of the Spirit (see John 3:5).

Don turned and began to retrace his steps. His own footmarks lay in the sand ahead, sharpened by the lengthening shadows of the setting sun. The old paths, he reflected. That was where he needed to walk. Was he in danger of straying?

"Be filled with the Spirit" (Ephesians 5:18). Now, there was a good text to ponder. "Go on being filled," was the force of Paul's Greek verb. Clearly the apostle reckoned that Christians could live in the realm of the Spirit without necessarily being immersed in him. Constantly they needed to keep on claiming and enjoying the fullness that was always there for the asking.

But where did speaking in tongues fit in? Was it the initial and infallible sign of being filled? Don knew this was the Pentecostal position. He also knew that Pentecostals are particularly fervent in embracing a gospel of salvation which is found in Christ alone. Nevertheless, he sensed a peril in their teaching. If tongues are the demanded proof of Spirit-baptism, and Spirit-baptism is necessary for a satisfactory and powerful Christian life, then sooner or later it will become desperately important to produce tongues. Certainty, status, acceptance, assurance: all begin to depend on something other than the work of Christ. That something, the New Testament teaches, is only granted to some. For Paul insists that to one is given through the Spirit one gift, to another, another gift and "to another, various kinds of tongues" (1 Corinthians 12:10). "Do all speak with tongues?" (1 Corinthians 12:30). No.

To his surprise Don found himself back at his cabin home. As he climbed into bed by the light of a paraffin lamp, with the singing of the seals and the murmur of the sea in his ears, he set his course for the remaining days of his all-too-brief retreat. He would read through Luke's Gospel at one sitting and the Acts of the Apostles at another. Avoiding all commentaries, he would simply allow the impact of Luke's two-part narrative to fall freshly upon him.

The following morning dawned fine and clear as Don sat on the verandah that opened directly on to the beach, and turned to Luke's opening words. Almost immediately the story gripped him. None of it was new, but the music of familiar incidents and phrases swept him along with new force and urgency. He followed the progress of the One whose first recorded words proclaimed him to be about his Father's work, and whose first public challenge presented a soaring symphony of praise and freedom, of comfort and salvation.

The Spirit of the Lord is upon me,
because he has anointed me to preach good news to the
    poor.
He has sent me to proclaim release to the captives
and recovering of sight to the blind,
to set at liberty those who are oppressed (Luke 4:18).

The Spirit of the Lord? Was this the key to the life of God's Son himself? Don turned back the page to recall how the very mystery of Christ's coming and birth were hidden in the secret activity of the Spirit.

The Holy Spirit will come upon you,
and the power of the Most High will overshadow you;
therefore the child to be born will be called holy,
the Son of God (Luke 1:35).

And the start of his public work? There it was again: "When Jesus . . . had been baptised . . . the Holy Spirit descended upon him in bodily form, as a dove . . . and Jesus returned in the power of the Spirit" (Luke 3:21,22; 4:14). Don turned on and on, noting how event after event in the life of Jesus was (from one point of view) a demonstration of the supernatural power of the Holy Spirit. The sun was well past its height before Luke's account was finished, and the rest of the day was spent in quiet thought and prayer.

Next day the sky was cloudless again ("I'm getting a tan, if nothing else!" thought Don), and it was time to begin Luke's second scroll. The famous first verse linked the two halves. "In the first book . . . I have dealt with all that Jesus *began* to do and teach . . ." (Acts 1:1). Luke implies that he will now recount what Jesus continued to do and teach! But Christ's first action is his ascension and return to heaven. Not to worry. His Spirit soon comes on the disciples, forms them into a church and empowers them to carry on the work. Through the church Jesus continues to act and teach.

Again, the familiar story came with fresh emphasis. The Holy Spirit was so pressingly present, so personally active at every step. He empowered Peter and the other disciples to preach with authority and conviction, to heal a cripple, defy temple guards, escape from prison, perform signs and wonders, set off on unlikely journeys to meet unexpected enquirers, see through hypocrisy, break out of traditional barriers, confront evil . . . The list went on. So intimate was the shared thought and purpose between Christian leaders and the Holy Spirit that after a hard argument among themselves they were able to say, in words of almost embarrassing familiarity, "It has seemed good to the Holy Spirit and to us . . ." (Acts 15:28).

Evening shadows were lengthening again as Don sank to his knees to face his personal dilemma. The Acts of the Apostles was the church's God-given handbook of order and evangelism. Brethren by upbringing, Baptist by choice and evangelical by conviction, he believed that without reservation. But the Acts not only promoted the kind of preaching he had long practised, and described the kind of conversions he had often witnessed. It also related (apparently as everyday events) frequent miracles, signs, healings and remarkable deliverances. These things were part of the normal experience of the early Christians. More, they were directly related to the early sharing of the good news.

Don prayed at length in silence, then got up stiffly and walked down to the sea. Shying a few stones across the waves, he pondered again. Cut the miraculous out of the Acts and you are left with a very tattered handbook. Leave it in, and the handbook finds little reflection in much of today's church experience. It seems about as much use as a do-it-yourself car-repair manual, which assumes you can lift the car off the ground with one hand while carrying out the repairs with the other!

All right. So some details of Pentecostal teaching leave serious question-marks behind. First- and second-class citizenship in the kingdom of heaven lurk there, with all their attendant dangers of pride, division, jealousy, introspection, manipulated emotion and self-induced 'proofs'. But are there not equal and opposite perils in main-line evangelicalism? Has not the wholesale rejection of the supernatural robbed Protestantism of half its power? Is it not an odd philosophy that proclaims faith in a supernatural Bible and a supernatural gospel, but rejects a supernatural life-style and supernatural evidence?

It was time to leave the remote cliff-top cabin, walk across the fields to the parked car, and drive home. No overwhelming emotional experience had marked the retreat, but many things were a good deal clearer. Could it be that many churches had lost their expectation of the miraculous, and then rationalised its absence? Could it be that people 'baptised in the Spirit' were using a confusing terminology to express their rediscovery of the supernatural implicit in the gospel? Could it be that what is objectively true of every follower of Christ (the fullness of the Spirit) often becomes subjectively experienced only later, as inhibitions are removed, expectation is heightened and latent gifts are brought to the surface and released? Could it be that, just as Christians need consciously to trust Christ for salvation, so they need equally consciously to trust the Holy Spirit to equip them for holy living, service and witness? Don could see no biblical objection to that, and a good deal of biblical confirmation of it. He returned to Sunderland determined on a policy of cautious and qualified openness to whatever new things God might wish to give.

So began a new journey of adventure and discovery. Relating it all fifteen years later could give a misleading impression. There was no dramatic change of direction, nor succession of startling incidents following one upon another. Sometimes weeks would pass without anything unusual happening. Certainly, the regular work of the church was pursued, and Don wavered in no way from his original conception of the task of the ministry. The Bible was still systematically expounded. We still longed above all else to see men and women converted to Christ. And we still measured spiritual progress in terms of growth in character and holiness, not in signs and wonders.

All that was new was a kind of flavour which permeated every activity. It was rather like the first touch of frost on a winter morning as you walk down the street. Nothing is visibly different, but there is a sparkle in the atmosphere, a crispness in the air you breathe, a tendency to square your shoulders, to breathe deeply and step out smartly, a desire to take a running slide along the pavement, a feeling that today anything could happen.

Anything could happen. That was the new factor. Sufficiently often, something did happen. There was no need to go looking for adventures. They were in the path, waiting to be enjoyed. The telephone, the mail, a personal call at the door – all would bring requests for help. The situation when investigated would call for some dramatic remedy, some specific intervention. And the voice of God seemed to whisper, 'There you are. Now I have granted one of my gifts to deal with that. Step out and trust me.'

Mrs Johnson showed many signs of genuine faith but was never seen at a Communion service. Don pointed out that she did not have to be a Baptist in order to receive Communion.

"Oh, it isn't that," she replied. "It's just that I cannot come."

"How do you mean?" Don asked, puzzled.

"Well, something just won't let me. I get my hat and coat on, and then somehow I can't move."

They walked together for a while, and she told Don more of herself. She had been widowed for several years and kept referring to the fact. As Don listened, two thoughts came into his mind persistently. So vivid were they that they almost presented themselves as pictures. One was the mental image of a lonely beach on which one solitary woman was walking. It was so realistic that he felt he could hear the waves breaking on the shingle. He had to blink to dismiss the picture. The other was simply one word 'spiritualism'. Could this possibly be the 'word of knowledge' spoken of by St Paul as one of the Holy Spirit's gifts? Was God telling Don the cause of his friend's problem? He drew a deep breath, and prepared to look a complete fool.

"Mrs Johnson, what happened at the seaside, and when did you get involved with spiritualism?" She looked thunderstruck, and then began to blush. The story tumbled out. When she was first widowed, she had gone to stay with relatives on the south coast. So great was her grief that she found herself bitterly resenting the married happiness of those with whom she lodged. Often she walked the beach alone and wrestled with her jealousy and self-pity. Returning home, she had invited a well-known medium into her house and tried to obtain proof that her husband was still alive in some other world. Some odd and impressive things had happened, and she became fascinated. Then she remembered her somewhat nominal faith, and decided not to pursue spiritualism any further.

"But what has all this to do with me, now?" she asked in bewilderment. "And what gave you the idea in the first place?"

"Look, I don't profess to understand it all," Don replied. "But I believe the root of your problem is here. The Bible

32

forbids dabbling in the world of spirits. God regards such things as an unhealthy dissatisfaction with what he has chosen in his wisdom to reveal to us, and what he has chosen to keep from us." He pulled out his pocket Bible, and showed Mrs Johnson the words of Isaiah: "When they say to you, 'Consult the mediums and the wizards who chirp and mutter', should not a people consult their God? Should they consult the dead on behalf of the living? To the teaching and to the testimony! Surely for this word which they speak there is no dawn" (8:19,20). "Now, you may not have meant to disobey God, Mrs Johnson, though by your embarrassment I think you must have suspected it. At any rate, you stepped out of God's will, and he was under no obligation to protect you from the consequences. There is evil in the spiritual world just as in the material world. I believe that it is an evil influence that is keeping you from Christian people, and from the Lord's Table. Look at what St Paul says about it: 'I do not want you to be partners with demons. You cannot drink the cup of the Lord and the cup of demons' " (1 Corinthians 10:20,21).

She looked thoroughly dismayed. "Whatever shall I do?" she asked.

This was the crunch! Don hesitated for a moment, and then plunged in. "Renounce the whole thing. Apologise to God for straying in forbidden paths. Ask him to forgive you. Then I will pray with you."

They knelt together and she spoke quite simply to God as Don suggested. He laid his hands on her head and claimed in prayer complete deliverance for her from any evil influence. Three days later she was present at the Communion service, her face alight with happiness. Not only had the strange physical restraint disappeared, but also her whole mental attitude had brightened and lightened. The 'cure' proved to be permanent.

A few weeks later, Don was asked by one of the church members to visit a neighbour. Janice was a pretty young housewife with a lovely home and a healthy family. She suffered from severe symptoms of depression, a black hopelessness which had no rational cause. A succession of tablets prescribed by her doctor produced side-effects as distressing as the illness. At a coffee morning held by our member she had shown a lot of interest in the meaning of the Christian Gospel.

They talked at great length, not about depression, but about Jesus Christ. Don left her with a copy of John's Gospel which she promised to read carefully. A week later he revisited her and found that Holy Spirit and holy scripture had worked together to bring her to a real understanding of her spiritual need, and a real desire to commit her life to Christ. They prayed together, a simple prayer of response to the Saviour's love, and thanked him for the new life which was his gift. Then Don asked for a bonus!

"Lord, you know the fears that oppress Janice. She feels so useless. She cannot take the pressures of life. But she is your child now. Lift this darkness and banish these fears, and demonstrate that you are Lord."

When Don visited Janice again a week later she was radiant. So different was her whole appearance that one neighbour had asked who her new doctor was! As the months went by, Janice proved to have other very deep problems, some of which stemmed from other people who had no desire to be helped by God. But without doubt, a corner was turned that day.

An obsessive addiction healed, a spiritual oppression broken, an emotional depression lifted: on each occasion new resources had been provided sufficient for the new demands with which we were being confronted. What else might God have in store? What other gifts might he be willing to display in response to simple, believing faith? His answer was nearer than we thought.

CHAPTER 4 – THE POWER TO HEAL

"Mary Clayton's been healed!" announced Margaret to David one Saturday morning as she came in from the shops. "It happened at the meeting at Richard's and Brenda's last night!"

Mary was captain of our Girls' Brigade company. A single lady in middle life, small, plump, apple-cheeked, with a cheerful but shy nature, she was the stuff of which so many English churches are made. A glutton for hard work, greatly concerned for the welfare of teenage girls, a tireless visitor in the nearby flats, she was one of the few church members who really got through to the local residents and disarmed their suspicions. On one of several occasions when the church was burgled by local youngsters, the equipment stolen included Mary's own record-player, on loan to the Brigade. When word passed around that she was the owner, that one item was quietly brought back and deposited at the church door!

Now Mary was having problems with a varicose ulcer on her right leg. After troubling her for several years, its condition suddenly worsened, and it became very painful and worrying. Her doctor warned that she must give up most of her voluntary activities if she was to be fit enough even to stumble painfully to work. Certainly she must resign her leadership of the Brigade.

Mary and Don discussed this at great length. How could Mary just give up the work to which God had called her? How could God want her to, anyway? Having given her the work amongst the girls, surely God did not want it to cease because of a varicose ulcer! "I shall pray about it for a month, and then come to the special prayer-meeting and ask for healing," she declared at last.

The crunch again! Dare we pray for complete healing?

The month ran its course and a dozen or so folk gathered in Richard's and Brenda's lounge. In the company was a prominent general practitioner from the city of Durham. He examined the leg and pursed his lips. Pus oozed from the front, the leg was swollen, and the skin over a large area was badly affected. "Even if the ulcer were to clear up and not worsen, the whole area would need a skin graft," he remarked glumly.

The meeting took its usual course. The Bible was read, God was thanked for all his gifts and praised for his salvation. One and another suggested a devotional chorus to sing, quoted a psalm and led the rest in simple, spontaneous words of thanksgiving. Gradually, the worshippers moved from praise to petition, sharing with God their concern for various problems, naming before him particular people in distress.

Suddenly, the doctor stood up and addressed Mary quietly. "I believe God is saying to you, 'Go in peace, your faith has made you whole.' " There was a hush in the room. Don crossed to Mary and signalled to Brenda to join him. She touched Mary's leg while he laid his hand on her head: "Dear Father, just do your perfect will, as we trust you. In the name of Jesus Christ. Amen."

When Mary removed the bandage the following morning to change the dressing there was a startling improvement. The whole area of destroyed flesh had grown over with the healthy pink of fresh tissue. The inflammation had gone. Only from a small sore spot at the front pus still oozed. Radiant with joy, Mary walked on air to the shops, where Margaret became the first to learn her glad news.

The small sore, however, remained a puzzle. A week passed, and the condition remained the same; no pain, flesh healed, but a continuing leakage of pus from that one place. We were grateful . . . and perplexed.

At the end of the week, Don had a visit from one of the Girls' Brigade lieutenants who assisted Mary. She was embarrassed and hesitant, but felt she had something to tell which worried her. "As you know, I was at the prayer-meeting last week. When you signalled to Brenda to pray

36

with Mary, I had the absurd feeling it should have been me, not her. But I know that's silly. I'm not a marvellous Christian at all, and I've never thought of such a thing before."

"Come on," Don said, and grabbed his coat. They drove straight to the church where Mary was busy as usual. "Now, lay your hand on the place while we all pray," he urged the lieutenant. Hesitantly, she did so. Mary removed the bandage, and found that the healing was complete. It has remained so over the years. The following month, at the next prayer-meeting, the Durham doctor declared, "What has happened makes no kind of medical sense."

The story of Mary's healing is typical of hundreds which have come out of the charismatic movement over the last twenty years. Yet, despite dramatic books from Kathryn Kuhlman and measured 'how-to-do-it' manuals from Agnes Sandford, Jim Glennon and others, healing still remains one of the most controversial aspects of the movement as the church enters the eighties.

That sickness and disease are two of the results of the Fall is clearly implied throughout the Bible. Pain in childbirth is specifically mentioned (Genesis 3:16), but the frequent connection made in the Old Testament between plague, pestilence and the judgment of God makes it clear that other illnesses are included as well.

Therefore it is not surprising to find healing and forgiveness from sin inextricably combined in the unfolding biblical story of God's grace and renewal towards fallen humanity. "If you will diligently hearken to the voice of the Lord your God, and do that which is right in his eyes, and give heed to his commandments and keep all his statutes, I will put none of the diseases upon you which I put upon the Egyptians; for I am the LORD, your healer" (Exodus 15:26).

> Bless the LORD, O my soul,
>   and forget not all his benefits,
> who forgives all your iniquity,
>   who heals all your diseases (Psalm 103:2,3).

Equally, from the beginning of his public ministry, Jesus went all over Galilee, "teaching in their synagogues and preaching the gospel of the kingdom and healing every disease and every infirmity among the people" (Matthew 4:23). Healing was integral to his redemptive work, "to fulfil what was spoken by the prophet Isaiah, 'He took our infirmities and bore our diseases' " (Matthew 8:17). So when the apostles preached the good news about Jesus, time and again they healed the sick in demonstration of the Spirit and of power. Down through the centuries Christians have cared for the sick, using every natural means at their disposal, but when God has moved in revival, supernatural healing has been seen as well.

The Bible also makes it clear that God's healing is not confined to physical illness and disease.

> He heals the brokenhearted,
> and binds up their wounds (Psalm 147:3).

When four friends carried a paralysed man to Jesus, the first words spoken were about the forgiveness of sins (Mark 2:5). But physical healing was very quickly linked to spiritual peace: "Rise, take up your pallet and go home . . . that you may know that the Son of man has authority on earth to forgive sins" (Mark 2:11,10).

From the disappearance of Mary's varicose ulcer we learned a great deal. Prayer had an obvious place. So did Mary's faith. It seemed to be given to her to believe, to such an extent that we felt cornered by her faith.

We learned, too, that God wanted to use us as a team, each with his or her part to play. The healing was not completed until the lieutenant discovered and exercised her own gift. What God seemed to be looking for was a company of people who offered themselves for his service, willing to be used together, individually, or not at all, as he saw fit. Our part was to care, to feel and to pray, to be sensitive to what God wanted to do. There was no room for self-display. Jealousy would have been absurd.

The same lessons were underlined when Marion's problem was raised. Marion was a middle-aged mother and a member of a nearby Presbyterian church. Her constant, nagging problem was gynaecological. Some chemical imbalance resisted every effort of medication and minor surgery to readjust. Her family doctor had long since handed her on to a consultant of high repute who also happened to be an elder in her church. All to no avail.

"I'm afraid that last treatment really was the last," the consultant confided sadly one day. "I've no fresh ideas. We've run through the lot. You'll have to live with it."

'Living with it' involved coming to terms with a crushing lassitude which made even the lightest housework a grim burden, and typing (Marion's employment) completely impossible. "I just cannot put the words together. They get totally scrambled," she explained.

Doctor and patient paused. "Look," Marion asked. "You know Mr Bridge at the Baptist church? Would you and he consider praying for me in a special way? I've heard things . . ."

Medical specialist and minister consulted, and agreed to pray separately for a month. The house-group was asked to pray, too. Then one spring morning the two men visited Marion. Pale sunshine slanted through the French windows, and birds chattered in the garden as the three read together from the Psalms. Then they read the story of the timid woman with the embarrassing gynaecological problem who pushed through the crowd to Jesus, "touched the fringe of his garment; and immediately her flow of blood ceased" (Luke 8:44).

"Jesus must have understood how sensitive she would feel," the doctor observed, "but he insisted on bringing the thing out into the open. No slipping away with a half-assurance of a half-understood bit of magic – 'I touched his coat, and was well' – none of that – she had to understand that faith was the life-line and the love of Jesus was the source. Read it, Marion."

Marion read, "And when the woman saw that she was

39

not hidden, she came trembling, and falling down before him declared in the presence of all the people why she had touched him, and how she had been immediately healed. And he said to her, 'Daughter, your faith has made you well; go in peace' " (Luke 8:47, 48).

Don, with half an eye on a sermon outline, murmured, "Not her touch but her trust. Not her feeling but her faith. Not impersonal power but a personal promise."

The room was suddenly very still. The birds had stopped their gossip. The splash of sunlight seemed to have brightened on the carpet. Doctor and pastor looked at each other, and together drew a deep breath. A quiet prayer, the laying on of hands, three figures kneeling together in the sun-dappled room, and the thing was done. Within hours Marion was typing. Every symptom had gone. The consultant was professionally obliged to keep the patient on his list for twelve months, but there was no more treatment, for none was needed. Quarterly visits simply confirmed that the trouble had ended. With abundant energy to spare, Marion became active in her church, and saw her husband and daughters commit themselves to Christ. When further expansion of the Baptist work led to a branch church being formed, Marion took on the daunting task of the women's leadership.

On the basis of these experiences, three local doctors, leaders in different churches, became convinced that expectant prayer with the laying on of hands should be part of a Christian doctor's regular practice. Thus, the renewal of faith and expectancy spilled over into a Church of England church, a Presbyterian church and a Brethren assembly. The snowball was growing and gathering momentum as it rolled down the hill.

Modern psychiatry has discovered that many physical illnesses and nervous disorders are rooted in past emotional hurts. Guilt, bitterness and pain are sometimes buried deeply in the subconscious mind. Did Jesus understand this when he forgave the paralysed man before he healed him? When these memories are brought to the cross of Christ, under the guidance of the Holy Spirit, then Christ's healing power may be seen in the body via the mind and the emotions.

Ron was a typical asthmatic. Round-shouldered, morose, over-defensive, a loner, he hung about on the outskirts of church life, never involved and always suspicious. Don recognised the type; he always did, because for years he had been that way himself. He was therefore very surprised when Ron registered for the next series of baptismal instruction classes. The lessons fascinated him; the sheer logic of Pauline doctrine, the unanswerable certainty of the man who finds himself chosen, called, pardoned and promised heaven, the calm assumption of certainty that the Bible displays as a record, not of man's insights, but of God's actions and words. In his case, without any special counselling or pastor-to-person prayer, Ron simply became a different person in the course of twelve weeks. His amazed parents attributed remarkable powers to a pastor who, in fact, had done nothing but let the good news speak for itself. There was a lesson in that, too. The healing was gradual, not immediate. Nor did it depend on the laying on of hands, for it was never employed.

Healing can be even slower. God never barges his way into his children's lives. He deals with them as individual people. It can take years to uncover one layer after another of shame, hurt, subterfuge and guilt. Each stage may need an act of healing for itself. Identifying the nature of the problem may require as much charismatic exercise as dealing with it. Disappointments and setbacks are hardly surprising. They certainly do not cast doubt on the reality of divine healing, any more than disappointing conversions compromise the truth of the gospel.

Bill was converted in the way evangelists delight to relate. A fellow pigeon-fancier had brought him to the church, and the change in him was almost instantaneous – at a certain level, that is. He stopped swearing, abandoned the public-house, and began to read the Bible with the astonished excitement of a total newcomer. But two things lingered for several years. One was a very volatile temper. The other was an irrational fear of illness and death. The

41

first created obvious problems within the fellowship, and the second seemed to deny one of the fundamentals of the faith he so eagerly embraced.

Don was puzzled, and shared his dismay with Richard who, as the one who had initiated the renewal at Enon, had become a kind of spiritual consultant. Richard had been reading about the complexity of those successive layers of subconscious hurt. Don had been fascinated by a true case of tri-personality, popularised in *The Three Faces of Eve*. Both had been pondering on the fact that Jesus Christ, the eternal Son of God, is unrestricted by time, since he dwells in eternity. "Jesus Christ is the same, yesterday and today and forever" says the writer to the Hebrews (13:8).

"C.S. Lewis suggests that, if we humans move along a straight line from past through present to future," said Don, "then we should think of God as a circle that contains the whole of the straight line at once."

"Hold on. That surely means something rather special," interrupted Richard. "If the past is still present with Christ, then perhaps he can move into a past situation now, and prevent it happening . . . well, no – not quite that, but you see what I'm getting at."

"I think we'd better pray about it," said Don. So they did. Next day Don pondered again on Bill's emotional problem. "Something happened years ago. This is the result. If we could help him to imagine Christ in that situation when it happened . . . going into it now, so to speak. But what situation?"

Don prayed again. A word came into his mind. It was a very embarrassing word. He dismissed it, but it kept coming back. He climbed into his car and drove across to Bill's house. As there was no possible way to be tactful about it, he took Bill aside and simply said the word. Bill began to tremble. He poured out a story which, until that moment, his conscious mind had resolutely refused to remember.

When Bill was a young boy, an uncle had made sexual advances to him. The frightened boy ran away and told no one, but loathed his uncle from that day forward. A little later, the man died. The boy was made to look at his uncle in the coffin (exactly as in *The Three Faces of Eve*). Staring at the corpse, he was filled with glee that his uncle was dead . . . and then appalled at the thought. Any psychiatrist could piece together the rest of the story. A boy growing to manhood had carried the hidden conviction that he was to blame for his uncle's death. Had he not wished it and gloated over it?

Here was the situation into which Jesus could come. "The same yesterday and today and forever," he could come *now* into Bill's *then*, and sponge it away. They knelt and asked him. The fear of death was washed away.

The violent temper was something else. Quarrels became too numerous, and Bill found another church in which to start again. Complete wholeness had not yet been found. How can it be, this side of the return of Christ and the completion of our redemption?

CHAPTER 5 – PROBLEMS AND QUESTIONS

Modern 'charismatic miracles' raise two questions. First, are the works of healing such as those we described in the previous chapter comparable to the acts of Jesus and the apostles which are recorded in the New Testament? Second, why are some healed and not others?

Don quickly faced the first problem when he was asked to speak to a group of Christian doctors about the healing ministry which was developing at Enon. He went armed with technical details from the doctors who had been involved in the incidents we have described. Yet, to his surprise, members of his audience were not easily persauded. Some even seemed to see the whole idea as a threat.

"There's no control experiment in all this," complained one. "The interesting fact that Mrs Smith has improved means absolutely nothing to a scientist. Did you have a hundred Mrs Smiths with the same disease who were prayed for? And another hundred who were not prayed for? What proportion of the first hundred and the second hundred recovered?"

"All right, all right, I take your point," laughed Don. "Look, the prayer meeting is not a scientifically-proven alternative to penicillin and cortisone. It is simply the place to which the Christian instinctively turns for strength and grace. It isn't a treatment; it's a way of opening his life to the help of God, exercised as God wills."

The chairman became so excited that he asked permission to make a speech himself. "In a long practice I have never seen a Bible miracle," he declared. "When Jesus dealt with a blind patient, he didn't improve a little; he saw. When Jesus touched a cripple, he didn't limp rather better than he used to; he took up his bed and walked. I must insist that, if we are talking about a healing comparable with those in Scripture, it must fulfil the following conditions. The disease must be organic, not psychosomatic. It must be incurable by natural means. It must be instantly healed, not gradually. The healing must be complete, not partial. And it must be permanent, not temporary. I have never, in all my observation of Pentecostalism, seen a so-called healing which fulfils these criteria."

There was a murmur of approval. Don was clearly not winning.

"All right, again," Don acknowledged. "But the demands you are making not only cannot be met by modern charismatics, but also they cannot be met by the Bible miracles, either. When did Jesus conduct a control experiment with a hundred paralytics? What evidence is there that the leprosy he healed is the modern 'incurable disease'? The word used simply means a disfiguring skin ailment. Isn't there at least a hint that some illnesses were psychosomatic? 'Your sins are forgiven' (Mark 2:5). 'Sin no more, that nothing worse befall you' (John 5:14). And how about this for a gradual cure? 'I see men; but they look like trees, walking' (Mark 8:24)."

Don looked around the excited audience. "You are all men who know the Bible well. Can someone recite to me the actual words used to describe miracles in the New Testament?" With a bit of prompting, it was done:

teras, a wonder, a marvel, something producing astonishment. The emphasis is on the effect on those who watched.
semeion, a sign, a mark, token, of miracles and wonders regarded as signs of a divine authority. Usually the word is used to denote the divine authority of Christ, or of the one performing the miracle.
dunamis, power, might, strength. The word underlines the origin of the miracle and its effectiveness. It happens because God does it.
ergon, a deed, action. The word emphasises divine gra-

ciousness and initiative. As if to say, "From such a God, what would you expect?"[1]

"Now," argued Don, "I maintain that none of that demands the criteria our chairman has imposed. God is not saying, 'See, I can do what doctors and hospitals cannot do.' He is saying, "See, I am gracious and loving. I know your needs. I am building my kingdom. Jesus Christ is saviour and king.' "

He paused for breath, and looked around again. Some were pensive. Some were grinning. Some were shaking their heads.

"You all know the astonishing effect that a few days of nourishment supplied by Tear Fund can have on people suffering from *kwashiorkor*. That comes as a wonder and a sign in the name of Christ. I've told you of a varicose ulcer that disappeared in the presence of two doctors. I also know what you as Christian physicians achieve through skill and dedication. I rejoice in both, as signs of the compassion of Christ.

"I personally suffered the misery of bronchial asthma for fourteen years. I was cured in a month by a Brethren homeopathic practitioner (sorry, but it's true!) who prayed with me. Afterwards, my own doctor said, 'Well, of course, asthma is only psychosomatic.' But why 'only'? He could do nothing for me in fourteen years. What's 'only' about that? My healing released my personality and helped to make me a preacher. As far as I'm concerned, in that healing the kingdom of God came to me."

Don sat down, and the meeting closed. No one won, for there was nothing to win. They all had to go back to a suffering world and a church under attack. They all had to return to Christian work suspended between the triumph of Christ's 'already achieved' at Calvary and Pentecost, and the eventual 'glorious liberty of the children of God' (Romans 8:19).

But the doctors' dilemma points towards the answer to the second problem: why are some healed in answer to prayer, and not others? Not only doctors, but also everyone in the West, to some extent, has been trained in scientific method for the past one hundred and fifty years. The overall effect of this has been to assert that what cannot be 'proved' by scientific observation is not real, and should be dismissed. The general conclusion has been that miracles do not happen any more, nor should we expect them to. But God heals in response to faith. If we do not believe he will heal, we are not likely to see miracles of healing.

Here is one reason why God often seems to take so long to heal, and why the healing comes in fits and starts. Because our faith is small, God only heals little by little, so as to strengthen our weak faith. The church in the West faces a whole crisis of confidence in this area. Conditioned by 'scientific' presuppositions, Christians need their total way of thinking to be reversed. In the third world there is no such problem. There, miracles of healing happen with a normality and a frequency which we in the West find breathtaking. For third-world Christians live in cultures where people expect a supernatural God to work supernaturally. If he did not, he would lose credibility.

But these answers do not solve the whole problem. For God does not heal only in response to faith. He also heals in mercy and grace in order to demonstrate his love in a suffering and fallen world. And at the end of the day his activity does not depend on actions of men, but on his own eternal purpose and plan. He is the Lord, and he will do it.

Sickness and disease may not be part of God's intention for his world, but neither is sin. Christ may have died for our infirmities and borne our diseases (see Matthew 8:17). He also bore our sins in his body on the tree, that we might die to sin and live to righteousness (see 1 Peter 2:24), yet sin remains an ever-present problem to the earth-bound Christian.

Every writer of every book on healing we have read admits, somewhere, that not everyone for whom they and their helpers have prayed has been healed. And to explain their disappointments, these writers fall back on what an older generation of Christians called, 'the secret will of God.' God is not the author of sin and suffering, neither is it his revealed will that they should continue in the world. But for reasons best known to himself, he displays his healing and saving power to some and not to others, and man cannot question why.

Jesus did not heal all who were sick. At the pool of Bethzatha "lay a multitude of invalids, blind, lame, paralysed", but Jesus healed only one of them, and he had been ill for thirty-eight years (John 5:3). Nor did Jesus always heal completely. Ten lepers were cleansed, but only one was made whole (see Luke 17:11-19, King James and English Revised Versions).

Nor does Jesus always heal in the way we think he should. Because he is the Son of God, he knows what is best, and the process of healing often takes a different path from the one we envisage. Enid was stricken with multiple sclerosis ten years ago and became desperately ill. Over the years as the church prayed, a measure of healing was given. Her sight and speech were restored and the use of her upper limbs. Feeling returned to the rest of her body, yet she was still confined to her wheelchair. When she received the laying on of hands publicly at a Communion service, the immediate effect was to restore her determination to get out and about, and to live as normal a life as possible, without just sitting complacently at home.

Shirley suffered from searing pains in her back from an accident at a Keep Fit class three years before. Despite endless visits to doctors, hospitals and osteopaths, she grew no better and became appalled at the thought of future total disability. Then she shared her problem with her minister. After several sessions of prayerful, careful counselling he persauded her to bring her need to the church. One night, in the prayer meeting, she spoke stumblingly and falteringly of her physical problem. During the prayers that followed, she received the laying on of hands, and healing was claimed in the name of Jesus. Nothing apparently happened. The pain remained as intense and restricting as ever. But about ten days later Shirley was overwhelmed with the love of God while she was alone at home. Beside herself with joy, she longed to telephone her friends and just share with them her sense of God's precious love. She hesitated, however, fearing they would think her a fool. Then the telephone rang in her own home and she was able to share her joy with the friend who had called and who did not think her a fool at all!

From that day forward, Shirley's life was transformed. Despite her physical disability she became tireless in helping others and in witnessing of the Saviour's love. Despite the pain, her face assumed a new tranquillity. If you like, she had been baptised with the Spirit, and the Spirit who glorifies Jesus filled her life with Jesus, too. Something else began to happen, as well. Shirley's back began to improve. At first, some days were better than others, and there were many setbacks. She continued receiving hospital treatment for many more months. But the church continued to pray, and John, the minister, would often lay his hand on her head with a simple prayer for healing as he gave her the bread at the Communion rail. Today, the hospital treatment is ended, and only an occasional twinge of pain reminds Shirely of the fate she once feared.

Don himself slipped and fell while working in open-air evangelism. He injured his back permanently. Ever since, intense pain has laid him low, sometimes for days and weeks at a time. Often, his injury has seemed to hinder his effectiveness, yet repeated prayer, alone and with others, has not brought healing. On the other hand he has found that elation and pride in a dozen disguised forms have crept into his ministry and hindered it . . . until, on his back and in some pain, he has learned humility once more. With Paul, he has learned to say, "I will all the more gladly boast of my weaknesses, that the power of Christ may rest upon me . . . When I am weak, then I am strong" (2 Corinthians 12:9,10).

Six weeks before her wedding Michelle was admitted to hospital for a seemingly straightforward appendectomy. To his dismay, the surgeon found instead a cancerous growth. After the operation he pronounced Michelle cured and she went ahead with the marriage. Yet within two years she was receiving further treatment as cancer continued to ravage her slim, frail body. Despite the fervent prayers of the church, no physical healing was seen. Yet Michelle's radiant joy and continuing service for Christ became an inspiration to all who knew her. "I can do all things in him who strengthens me" (Philippians 4:13) became her favourite verse of Scripture, as in the remaining months of her brief life she applied its truth in a score of different ways. People marvelled at her husband Gordon's patience and tenderness in caring for her. Her middle-aged parents found a strength and fortitude to face the trial of which they had never dreamed. Towards the end Michelle suffered a stroke which impaired her speech. Her thin, wrinkled face made her look twice her age. Yet she never lost her joy or peace in Christ. Today, Michelle is completely whole. She lives and reigns with Christ where there is no more pain (Revelation 21:4). In life and in death, in answer to the prayers of his people, Jesus was displayed and glorified.

There is no final answer to the question why some are healed and not others. The Bible instructs us to pray for the sick that they may be healed. Jesus sends us to preach and to heal in his name. He encourages us to believe, and promises to answer according to our faith. But at the end of the day we must leave the issue with him, and with his loving purpose and care.

Back in Sunderland, Mary's healing marked a turning point in the life of the church. Hitherto, the renewal of Enon had been a fairly quiet affair. Most of the incidents recorded thus far had been known only to Don and to one or two others. Mary's eager testimony ended all that. What was happening now had to be faced by a wider circle of folk than before. In some ways the problems were just beginning.

Notes

[1] Definitions of Greek words are taken from G. Abbot-Smith, *A Manual Greek Lexicon of the New Testament* (T. & T. Clark. 3rd ed., 1937).

CHAPTER 6 – WHEN THE SPIRIT COMES

"Richard, what are these meetings you've started holding in your home?" Richard was sitting with David and Margaret, and David was asking deliberately awkward and provocative questions. Immersed in the busy and exhausting routine of teaching, marking and preparation, learning to live as husband and wife, delighted in just enjoying each other and their new home, David and Margaret had been largely ignorant of many of the events recorded so far. Each Sunday they gladly worshipped at Enon. When schoolwork permitted, they attended the prayer-meeting as well. For the first time in their lives they belonged to a growing church, and rejoiced at the numbers who filled the pews week by week. But when they heard of the meetings at Richard's and Brenda's, of the baptism of the Spirit and of speaking with tongues they were horrified. What was happening at Richard's and Brenda's was typical, they thought, of the subtle way the Devil attacked growing churches and brought their work to nothing.

"They're meetings for prayer and for the exercise of God's gifts. We ask God to fill us with his Spirit and to use us as he wills," Richard quietly replied.

"Richard, that's Pentecostalism and you know it! You'll split the church! All this blessing under Don's ministry and now this! We've seen it all before. There was this church in Sheffield with a new minister just like Don. Lots of people were converted and things were really going well. Then one weekend the young people went off to a meeting somewhere and came back speaking with tongues. Soon they were denouncing the minister and other leaders because they weren't filled with the Spirit. Then they cleared off to a Pentecostal church and took half the congregation with them. What's really sad is that most of them aren't even following Christ today."

"Our meetings aren't Pentecostal meetings, David," Richard replied, unperturbed. "They're quite different. Why don't you come and see for yourselves?"

"Oh, I don't know. It's all emotionalism! I went to this meeting once, addressed by one of the Jefferies brothers. You've never seen anything like it! He just knew how to whip everybody up into a state, and he did it quite deliberately, two or three times during the course of the evening. You should have heard the noise when he got everybody going, praying all at once, shouting at the tops of their voices. They needed to learn to do things decently and in order."

"I've got this girl at school," Margaret interjected. "She's in my sixth-form group doing A level RE. She was doing ever so well, but now she's stopped working altogether. She's started going to the Pentecostal church and they've told her church activities are more important than homework. What's really disturbing, though, is the way she's trying to be baptised in the Spirit. She's in a terrible state, fasting and praying, all because she can't speak in tongues."

"Our meetings aren't noisy and emotional," Richard replied. "They're quiet and orderly. You come and see for yourselves."

"Anyway, these gifts of prophecy and tongues, and the other supernatural gifts we read about in the Bible," David went on. "We've always been taught they were just given for the New Testament period, a sort of 'blast-off' to launch the church into orbit. That's what Paul says, isn't it? 'As for prophecies, they will pass away; as for tongues, they will cease'" (1 Corinthians 13:8).

"Yes, Paul does say that," Richard answered. "But when does Paul say that will happen? You have a look and see."

For the first time David felt unsure of himself. Brought up in a Christian home, taught the Bible ever since he could remember, qualified in theology, he thought he knew

52

God's word inside-out. He was usually the one showing people what the Bible taught, not the other way round. "Mm," he admitted ruefully as they looked again at 1 Corinthians 13. " 'When the perfect comes' " (verse 10).

"Has that happened yet?" Richard asked quietly.

"No, I don't suppose it has . . . Anyway, I still don't like it," David continued, stubborn to the last. "You're holding these meetings. They're unannounced. You invite a select circle of friends. You'll bring trouble in the church."

"Anyone can come," Richard rejoined, "and you're specially invited."

So it was that with very mixed feelings David and Margaret pedalled their tandem across the town to Richard's and Brenda's the following Friday evening. They were physically and mentally tired after another exhausting week at work. They were very, very dubious about the whole affair. On their arrival they were welcomed warmly and were somewhat relieved to spot some familiar faces. Mary was there, rejoicing in her leg which had been healed the month before. New friends were introduced. David and Margaret squatted on the floor in the already overcrowded room.

The meeting started normally and quietly enough. Someone read a passage from the Bible and the people spent the next twenty to thirty minutes commenting in turn on what it said and what it meant in their situation. David relaxed. He was on familiar ground, and he made one or two comments himself. Then the people began to share their needs among themselves, asking for prayer for their own and others' needs. Then the prayers began.

Once again, the procedure was normal and familiar. One and another prayed, simple prayers of thanksgiving, brief prayers of petition. Then, there was silence. David had known meetings like that before, often. One or two would pray, then an embarrassed silence would follow. After a while, someone would say another awkward prayer, to keep the meeting going, then silence again. But this silence was different. It did not seem to matter that no one was praying aloud. No one felt embarrassed. In the silence, which perhaps lasted for the next ten to fifteen minutes, Richard's and Brenda's room was filled with the presence of God in a startlingly real and indescribable way. David and Margaret had never known anything like it. Don had, in some of the Brethren Communion services he had enjoyed in his childhood and youth. Doubtless, Quakers and contemplative Catholics would have found the experience quite familiar. But for David and Margaret it was totally new. Tiredness and exhaustion were forgotten as they quietly enjoyed God for himself. Anything more different from noisy emotionalism could not have been imagined.

Finally, Don broke the silence. But what he said was new and different, too. He did not pray in quite the normal way. During the silence, a phrase had begun to run through his mind. Again and again it came. Finally, he was impelled to speak. Feeling exceedingly foolish, he broke the silence and said aloud, "The Lord stands high over the earth." No sooner were the words uttered than another sentence was pressing on his attention: "The whole world is beneath his feet." Before he had said the word 'feet', the next words were there: "His enemies are like grains of sand, caught up in his hand, and trickling between his fingers." With growing confidence he carried on:

"Great though the problems seem to you they are
    nothing to him.
In your foolishness, bow to his wisdom.
In your weakness confide in his strength.
In your ignorance, trust in his knowledge."

"So that's prophecy," thought David. "Nothing wrong with that." Then someone else began, as David feared they would, speaking not in English but in words of an unknown tongue. When David had heard this phenomenon previously, he had always been profoundly disturbed. Something about it had just not rung true. He had consistently argued that, if the gift were genuine, then, whether it was familiar or not, it should sound appropriate and right, and in

54

David's experience it never had. But again, this was different. The speaker was an attractive girl student from Newcastle, already making a dramatic impact on everyone she met with her radiant testimony to Christ. The sounds she uttered were beautiful, poetic, and although they did not understand a word, everyone present had no difficulty in recognising the language as a tongue of angels (1 Corinthians 13:1).

To David's surprise he was not the only sceptic in the meeting that night. A well-educated and widely-travelled man was there as well. He was suspicious of tongues and interpretation, too, and quietly decided to apply a little test. He reasoned to himself that a genuine language would betray linguistic form and shape which he should be able to pick out even though he did not recognise the language itself. Half of his mind was occupied with this, the other half with a personal problem which affected his business and his home, and which might make it necessary for him to move house, very reluctantly. He had wondered whether to share this with the group, but had decided not to do so.

When Jenny began to speak, the visitor listened carefully. It did seem to be more than mere babbling. It did sound as if there was a structure about it. Moreover, three successive sentences were either repetitions or nearly so. "Now then," he thought, "if the interpretation is genuine and not made up, there should come a repetition of three identical or nearly-identical phrases." After a few moments, someone duly gave an interpretation, and it included the following phrases:

> Commit your way to the Lord.
> Commit your work to the Lord.
> Commit your home to the Lord.

With a start, he realised that the looked-for repetition had come, and that it was addressed to him!

When the meeting finally ended, David and Margaret had no doubts. All their questions might not have been answered, but whatever was happening at Richard's and Brenda's was of God. They could hardly wait for the next meeting in four weeks' time.

Winter comes early in the north, and the frost bites hard. Don was sitting at his upstairs study desk, mind wandering, as he looked glumly at the white rime on the purple tiles of the roof across the street. The sky was a sullen grey with the tinge of yellow that threatens snow. His thoughts were wintry, too. A distasteful task lay ahead which threatened to make him many enemies.

Little signs going back as far as the previous spring had gradually forced Don's attention on to a developing relationship between two people within the circle of the church's activity. The relationship was fraught with destructive possibilities, and on any reading of the New Testament was divinely forbidden. To let it continue without a determined effort to warn and discipline would be pastorally irresponsible. Yet any accusation would be violently denied, and not only by the two people most immediately involved. Denied? Perhaps there was really nothing in it after all? No, there was no escape that way. A score of glances and gestures, a dozen remarks with double meanings, two or three cynical comments from non-church-going people in the district all added up to a total which Don's emotions rejected but which his mind insisted was inescapable.

Every pastor, everyone who cares about family life, has seen it before: the eventual, inevitable exposure; the white-faced, tearful wife, the last to suspect anything; the red-faced husband, half-defiant; the third point of the triangle; the gossip in the neighbourhood and the crippling of the church's witness as a result; another addition to the stock of anecdotes for everyone in the public-house and the hairdresser's who is pleased to have another reason for rejecting the local Christian presence.

Don shifted uneasily in his chair and flicked through the

pages of his Bible. But what was the point of that? He knew enough from the inspired handbook to realise that the problem must be tackled. He was not about to find some welcome passage which would assure him he need do nothing after all. He began to pray, a murmur of words addressed half to himself and half to God.

"Forgive me, Lord, for putting it off so long. You know why! I *hate* rows and confrontations. (The man is the key to this. If he would admit it and pull out now, she would cave in straight away.) Please grant me the strength to tackle this without any more delay, Lord. (Delay? Yes! There's been nothing physical yet, I'm sure of that. If only, if only . . . there's still time to save it.)

"Oh God, what can *I* do? I've asked *You* to intervene in power or in mercy, hitting them hard to stop them, or gently showing them the danger. You haven't done it. (If *I* tackle him, he could easily hit *me*. At the very least there'll be the most terrible quarrel. Is it libel, anyway? Or slander? I can never remember which is which.)

"All right, God. He drives home today. It's Friday. I'll visit him this evening and face him. But, *please* help me. *Please* make it go right."

Suddenly, still murmuring his half-prayer and half-soliloquy, Don was no longer using proper words, at least, not English words. He knew enough Latin to fail A-levels, and enough New Testament Greek to squeeze into the Baptist ministry, but these words were from neither of these, either. Gentle speech was flowing from his lips. There was no strong emotion, and certainly no compulsion. Don was talking, not someone else, but the words made no sense. Or rather, they meant something which he could feel and sense but could not define. The meaning hovered on the back edge of his mind – like that just-forgotten phrase which we say is 'on the tip of my tongue' – like that very vivid dream just slipping below the horizon of definition as you awake, still feeling its atmosphere.

Don's 'prayer' lasted perhaps two minutes, and then he stopped. He could have stopped sooner. In fact, he did stop once, and then started again. The words were somehow there, ready-shaped, inviting him to use them or not, as he wished. Now there were no more. He rose from his knees a little stiffly and gazed through the window at the purple tiles once more. Tears filled his eyes. He rubbed them away and noticed that the first, tiny flakes of threatened snow were beginning to fall.

Tears in his eyes, but joy in his heart! There was a great feeling of release and relief. The problem of the triangle was going to be solved. Indeed, it was solved already. Don merely had to go to the house that evening as he had promised, and all would be well. Then another thought came with a mild sense of surprise and curiosity: "I suppose I have been speaking in tongues!"

Don glanced at his watch – a few minutes past eleven – seven hours, at least, before the visit. The man he had to see would be about a hundred miles away visiting his Yorkshire circle of trade contacts. Ah, well, it was in God's hands. All was going to come out right. And it was Friday, with one of the Sunday sermons still unprepared.

By six o'clock the snow was falling steadily with a sense of purpose that suggested a long stay. The flakes flattened and melted against the windscreen as Don pushed cautiously westward from Sunderland along the rising Durham road. Soon, the headlights picked out the village to the left of the main road and he turned into the new housing estate. Things would be all right. But how would they be all right? "In thee, O Lord, do I put my trust."

Don's friend answered the door (he was his friend, and Don was his pastor). He sported a beautiful black eye, and looked white and drawn.

"Don! Come in! You're just the man I want to see! I wondered whether to ring you!"

He waved Don to a chair, and sat down himself and lit a cigarette with shaking fingers, waving it apologetically. "Sorry about this. I've given them up twice. But tonight I need one." He blew out a cloud of smoke, slowly, then stubbed out the cigarette with a quick gesture. "How long has it been snowing here? It started this morning in Yorkshire. My day for the North Riding, you know! Mid-morning, I got into a skid and finished up with the car wrapped round a pillar-box. Not worth trying to mend. A write-off, I guess."

He stood up, planting himself in front of Don. "Look, Don. I could have been killed. Front end mixed up with a pillar-box, and the car behind me followed my skid and finished up inside my boot. I could have had it. I climbed out in one piece" (he touched his cheek gingerly) "apart from this, and I was shaking like a jelly. And you know what my first thought was?"

Don rose, and gripped his elbows. "I think I can guess. You realised you might easily have been dead. And that means meeting God with the account-books open, including the account for your friendship with . . ." (and he spoke the name).

His friend sat down, heavily, head in hands, and began to sob. He cried in the way a man cries on those very rare occasions when he cries at all. Don let him cry it out, and asked quietly, "Is that what your first thought was?"

He nodded, silently, his face devastated. "More or less."

"And are you going to break it, now, without delay?"

This time he managed to speak. "Yes. Right away. I've been totally stupid. O Lord, what a fool . . ."

He wept more quietly this time, then lifted his wet face. "It never got anywhere, you know. But it would have done. Oh yes, it would have done. Well, not now. Not any more."

There would be more tears in another house that night, but no resistance. The key had turned, and the door was open.

Before Don left, he asked a final question. "Just when did you go into that skid this morning?"

"When? Mid-morning. Eleven o'clock, in fact, give or take a few minutes. Why?"

Don did not answer, but his heart sang as he drove home through the snow. Eleven o'clock! He had prayed desperately about an insoluble problem in words he did not understand. As he prayed, he knew his prayer was heard. A hundred miles away two cars went into a skid, and the problem was solved.

CHAPTER 8 – PUTTING IT TOGETHER

The quiet hubbub of conversation signalled the start of another Friday meeting in Richard's and Brenda's lounge. Greetings were exchanged as friends, old and new, gathered once more for worship and prayer, praise and ministry, under the direct leading of the Holy Spirit. Once again the Scriptures were read and comments exchanged on their meaning and application in today's world. Once again, Jesus was adored in simple words of loving praise. Needs, personal and for others, were humbly brought to the 'throne of grace'. And yet again the worshippers found themselves caught up to heaven in periods of deep, soaring silence, each in his own way simply enjoying the presence of the Father.

In the silence David found words which were not English coming into his mind and forming on his lips. He did not utter them audibly, then, or on subsequent occasions. But as he allowed the words to form, so his sense of God and his loving, strengthening presence was heightened, and the silence became more precious than ever. In the weeks that followed he was to find this new language of prayer invaluable in difficult situations, at work or when preparing to teach. It seemed to give him new power and effectiveness.

Not that David has always enthusiastically embraced the gift of tongues. His earlier reluctance about it remained even after he began to exercise the gift himself. He has often neglected it for months at a time. Until very recently he never used the gift aloud in the presence of any other Christian. Nor has the gift transformed his Christian life and solved all his problems. Indeed, to some extent it has had the opposite effect, although by making him more conscious of his problems it has prepared the way for inner healing and peace.

Because tongues are so apparently strange, they form an inevitable focus whenever charismatic renewal is discussed. Some modern translations of the Bible do not help the discussion. The *New English Bible*'s 'tongues of ecstasy' and the *Good News Bible*'s 'strange tongues', easily confirm people's worst suspicions. Yet as we have shown, the gift need not be associated with emotional excitement – and never was during our time in Sunderland. The Greek word simply means 'other languages'. Paul says these languages may be 'tongues of men and of angels' (1 Corinthians 13:1).

On the Day of Pentecost the 'other tongues' were human languages, for people from all over the world heard the apostles speaking in their native languages, declaring the mighty works of God (see Acts 2:5-11). When the new age of God's Kingdom dawned, human barriers were broken. For a brief moment, language barriers, themselves the results of human rebellion and pride, were ended (see Genesis 11:1-9). 'Pentecost was the Tower of Babel stood on its head.' Social and racial barriers fell, too, as rich and poor shared their possessions, and Samaritans and Gentiles were baptised in the name of Jesus.

Many modern 'tongues' are other human languages. Sometimes, someone present recognises the language and is usually amazed at its eloquence and beautiful expression. But in the New Testament the Pentecost experience was never quite repeated. At Caesarea and Ephesus there is no suggestion that foreigners recognised their own languages. At Corinth, an interpreter was always necessary. There, the gift served a threefold purpose.

First, it demonstrated the truth of God to unbelievers. In a surprising statement Paul declares, "tongues are a sign . . . for unbelievers" (1 Corinthians 14:23). He speaks in the context of a quotation from the Old Testament where God complains about his people. They will not listen to him or obey him. They have become, in effect, unbelievers. Time and again he speaks, but still they reject him. So he speaks "by men of strange tongues, and by the lips of foreigners," but "even then they will not listen" (1 Corinthians 14:21).

Some people will never respond to the Gospel. Truth will always be to them a nonsense, and so hearing Christians speaking in tongues confirms their worst fears. They always thought these folk were mad and now they are sure! So in public worship prophecy is always preferable to tongues. For God prefers mercy to judgment. He would rather encourage dawning faith than confirm determined unbelief. So, "if all prophesy, and an unbeliever or outsider enters . . . the secrets of his heart are disclosed; . . . falling on his face, he will worship God and declare that God is really among you" (1 Corinthians 14:24,25).

Secondly, at Corinth, tongues provided a verbal intimacy with God. "One who speaks in a tongue speaks not to men but to God," says Paul. "He utters mysteries in the Spirit" (1 Corinthians 14:2). "He who speaks in a tongue edifies himself . . . If I pray in a tongue my spirit prays" (1 Corinthians 14:4,14). This was exactly what David found in the silence at Richard's and Brenda's. Through tongues he enjoyed an identity with God at a deeper level than he had ever known before.

In a similar way this was what Don experienced when he prayed for help in dealing with the insoluble problem. Paul tells us that "the Spirit helps us in our weakness; for we do not know how to pray as we ought, but the Spirit himself intercedes for us with sighs too deep for words" (Romans 8:26). As Don prayed that winter's morning, the Spirit was already at prayer, for the people involved prayed with and through him. In another language Don prayed for a car crash to bring an erring Christian to repent. His natural mind would never have accepted that. His English language would have created a block because it would have built words which he could not accept. So God gave him another language to verbalise his longing and express God's promptings without the unacceptable words getting in the way. So, says Paul, "I will pray with the Spirit and I will pray with the mind also" (1 Corinthians 14:15). Like him, we and many others have found that a combination of natural and supernatural prayer builds us up and helps us to pray for others in need.

Thirdly, tongues (with interpretation) enabled the Christians at Corinth to function as a body. In Sunderland, this aspect of the gift was particularly well demonstrated in the meeting described in the previous chapter. There was a man with a domestic problem which he could and should have shared. Our student girl was sensitive enough to know there was a worry, but obviously had no information on which to base a sympathetic prayer. So she prayed in another language. The Divine Friend who had prompted her sympathy now prompted her words 'in tongues'. The release of her spirit from the need to know the situation became the release of her tongue and her compassion in non-cerebral but deeply-felt prayer.

But there were other people present. They too belonged to Christ's body, and they too should share in the experience of support and sympathy. So to one of them, also sensitive to the atmosphere, was given the ability to catch it and verbalise it, to 'interpret' it as one might interpret complicated music or an enigmatic painting to those who do not grasp the meaning. Surely, such an intimate sharing of concern and compassion, of need and of answer, is sufficient reason for the seemingly roundabout route of the prayer, "that there may be no discord in the body, but that the members may have the same care for one another. If one member suffers, all suffer together; if one member is honoured, all rejoice together" (1 Corinthians 12:25,26). "Therefore, he who speaks in a tongue should pray for the power to interpret" (1 Corinthians 14:13).

Does this then mean that all Christians should pray in tongues? Are the Pentecostals right, after all? Is every individual Christian life incomplete without the exercise of this divine prayer language? Paul indeed says, "I want you all to speak in tongues" (1 Corinthians 14:5), and he commands the Ephesian Christians to 'pray at all times in the Spirit' (Ephesians 6:18). But he is equally insistent that tongues is but one gift among many which are apportioned to different individual Christians by the Spirit as he wills (see 1 Corinthians 12:4-11). And he asks rhetorically, "Do all speak with tongues?" (1 Corinthians 12:30). His clearly implied answer is 'No'.

With Paul we naturally wish that all Christians should share the precious gift of God's prayer-language which the Spirit has given to us. We would suggest that all should be open to the exercise of the gift, and should ask God for it. But in our experience we know that many Spirit-filled Christians do not enjoy this gift, nor, so far as we can see, is their sensitivity in prayer and effectiveness in service in any way impaired thereby. Christians should never become 'hung-up' on this gift, overestimating its value and importance on the one hand or on the other becoming distressed at their lack of it. "Earnestly desire the higher gifts" (1 Corinthians 12:31) counsels Paul, before urging on his readers the 'more excellent way' of Christ-like, self-giving love which all should display (see 1 Corinthians 13).

Closely allied to tongues is the gift of prophecy, whereby the Spirit can speak directly to a church or to particular individuals without the intermediate stage of the divine prayer-language. Many are suspicious of this gift because they fear it compromises the finality of God's revelation of himself in Christ. This fear, however, is groundless. Prophecy, in the New Testament, never claims to add to the finality of the person and work of Christ. Nor indeed does it add to the Bible's witness to Jesus, either. It is simply a means whereby the Spirit applies God's revelation in Christ to particular needs and situations. That has always been necessary in every age of the church's life.

Traditionally, prophecy has been exercised through preaching. Sometimes preachers have addressed whole nations and generations through their prophetic proclamation of God's word. Such, for example, were John Chrysostom, the 'golden-tongued' elder at Antioch in the fourth century, George Whitfield and Charles Haddon Spurgeon in England in the eighteenth and nineteenth centuries. Dietrich Bonhoeffer, Billy Graham and Francis Schaeffer are possible modern examples of those who speak in this widespread, influential way. More often, God takes the general words of preachers and applies them with breathtaking directness to particular individuals who are present in the congregation.

"Don, I've discovered what prophecy is," a young engineer declared one day.

"Have you?" Don laughed. "I'd be interested to know!"

"Well, for the last month I have struggled against the realisation that I must become a Christian. Each Sunday I have come to church with mixed feelings, clinging to a succession of objections to Christianity. Each Sunday the sermon has dealt with that particular objection. Yet I told no one of my thoughts. Well, Don, I'm giving up the struggle. God can have me."

Bob married the woman who had brought him to church. They were baptised, became members, and subsequently gave up lucrative jobs to engage in residential welfare work amongst children.

In our informal prayer-groups we learned that prophecy is not the prerogative of preachers. Others can exercise the gift, as they speak simple words and phrases which God puts into their minds as they worship and pray to him. "You can all prophesy," says Paul, "one by one, so that all may learn and all be encouraged" (1 Corinthians 14:31).

The prophecies God gave in this way were generally addressed to the whole group, but time and again individuals would later testify to the particular relevance they had to them. The prophecies were also always couched in scriptural-type language. That was as it should have been, for prophecies which contradict God's word are never inspired by the Spirit. That is why, when two or three prophets speak, the others should weigh what is said, for the spirits of prophets are subject to prophets (see 1 Corinthians 14:29,32).

So the renewal at Enon continued to grow and spread as an increasing number of people received blessing through it and found through the gifts of the Spirit new abilities to minister to others. Hitherto, the renewal had taken place with little or no direct contact with Pentecostalism or with the newer charismatic movement which, by then, was sweeping the country. Now it was time to find out what God was doing beyond our four walls. Once again, Don went into retreat.

CHAPTER 9 – TRUE WORSHIP

For mile after mile the car soared effortlessly up the long hills on to the North York Moors. To the right, ridge upon ridge of silent, empty bracken and heather was broken only by the cultivated cups of Eskdale and Rosedale. To the left stretched the great horizon of the bleak North Sea. Its endless rollers tumbled and broke beneath the moss-covered ruins of Whitby Abbey, where Celtic and Roman Christianity had settled the date of Easter. Silver, sinister and monstrous on the hill-line ahead loomed the three giant golf-balls of Fylingdales. Their endless radar beams promise four minutes' warning of nuclear missiles from the east, long enough to dispatch equal destruction in return, and thus, it is hoped, to preserve the balance of terror.

Don was on his way to Scarborough to check the rather euphoric assertions of a growing number of Christians that God was doing a new thing, cutting through the traditions, hesitations and prejudices of his people, bringing new life through the charismatic movement. The road was new, too. Gone were the twists and turns, the hair-pin bends and the one-in-five gradients of Don's cycling youth. Valleys had been filled, hill-sides sliced apart, embankments built and streams culverted to make an easy way for the modern motorist. Was there a parable in that?

In the wilderness prepare the way of the LORD,
    make straight in the desert a highway for our God.
Every valley shall be lifted up,
    and every mountain and hill be made low;
the uneven ground shall become level,
    and the rough places a plain.
And the glory of the LORD shall be revealed (Isaiah 40:3-5).

68

So chanted the prophet, using an ancient dictator's command to build a new road for his triumphant progress as a picture of God's action in power and grace to bring rescue, renewal and reformation to his people. Was God fulfilling Isaiah's prophecy once more?

The old mansion perched on the hillside seemed a modest place for spiritual revival. The usual arrangements for religious conferences prevailed: semi-dormitory accommodation, plastic table-tops, alarmingly frequent carbohydrate meals, hurried walks around the gardens after too much sitting and listening. A fairly average mixture of Christians was there, too: Anglican curates in jeans and pullovers, free-church ministers in tweedy jackets, spinsters with cardigans draped over their shoulders, a Sir John Someone, secretary to a bishop, and a slightly bewildered Roman Catholic layman. He had reached Rome via disillusion with Christian Science, and asked politely in conversation one day if Methodists believed in the deity of our Lord! The three guest speakers were the Anglican founder of the Fountain Trust, an enthusiastic American Pentecostal who shocked his denomination by fraternising with the World Council of Churches, and a Methodist layman whose spiritualising and typology of Old Testament passages strongly reminded Don of his Brethren childhood.

There the resemblance to previous conferences ended. For there was an undefinable undercurrent of gentle excitement about the whole thing which occasionally broke through into a startling quality of worship or of intercessory prayer. A lecture on 'the ministry of deliverance' seemed to assume without much argument that any local church should be seeing miraculous healing and exorcisms. A Bible study on 'the inheritance of the saints in light' presupposed a joyous, almost intoxicated confidence in the potential in every Christian for victorious living. Immediacy was the only word to describe it all. A here-and-now encounter with God at the level of subjective experience was assumed to be the norm. It was not enough to say, "I know I am a child of God because the Bible assures me so", but one had to say, "I know it because my spirit leaps in response to the

69

Spirit of God in a deep, inward assurance that this is so."

Surprisingly, there was little talk about the Holy Spirit, except in one lecture. Jesus Christ was the central topic, his perfect atonement, his physical resurrection, his present rule at the Father's side, his continuing work in the church of sifting, searching, transforming, renewing, saving and healing. Everything was totally evangelical, scrupulously orthodox, in many ways completely familiar. Yet all the time that undercurrent of excitement was there, as if everyone was in on some new half-uttered secret.

Immediacy described the worship, too. Sometimes they worshipped when they were not particularly supposed to. On the second morning they stood to sing a hymn before settling down for a forty-minute lecture on *Counselling and Pastoral Care*. The words were familiar enough:

> Praise, my soul, the King of heaven,
> To his feet thy tribute bring.
> Ransomed, healed, restored, forgiven,
> Who like thee his praise should sing?

There was no warming-up session, no hearty exhortation from the chairman to, 'put your hearts into it'. But as they sang, the tremendous reality of what it meant to be ransomed, healed, restored, forgiven, swept over them. Still standing, they were led by the chairman in a quiet prayer of thanksgiving. When he said, 'Amen', no one sat down. Someone else began to pray, and then a third, pouring out gratitude and adoration to the Giver of all grace. Another guest struck up a four-line chorus, "How greatly Jesus must have loved me!" Someone else quoted a collect from the Book of Common Prayer. A man spoke in tongues and a woman interpreted. A hymn was suggested and sung from memory, then came another prayer and a five-minute silence punctuated by the quietest of murmurs, 'Thank you, Lord,' and 'Dear Father'. Someone read a psalm and someone else prayed again. So it continued, until, ninety minutes later, a rather hesitant conference-centre manager apologetically interrupted to point out that the luncheon-gong had sounded ten minutes ago. They 'came to' and found themselves still standing, almost too stiff to move. At that conference they never did learn how to counsel the distressed!

More consciously organised but no less spontaneous was the final Communion Service. This was built loosely around the Series Two Alternative Service which was agitating so many Anglicans at that time. The words were followed from the little grey booklets, through the various themes of adoration, intercession, confession, preparation, Communion and so on, but with something of a difference. Having praised God in the suggested words, they remained on that theme in impromptu prayer and singing for another fifteen minutes. They made their general confession in the appointed words, but then some present felt free to be more specific, and openly admitted the need for minor adjustments among themselves. Don found a Baptist minister's wife admitting that she had been irritated by his failure to reject infant baptism during a meal-time conversation on the previous day. He found himself confessing to the Catholic layman that it had taken him two days to 'forgive' him for the cruelties of the Spanish Inquisition.

So it continued, in the same fascinating, half-structured and half-extempore manner, sometimes just very gently guided into the next phase by the chairman. In the petitions and intercessions some asked in detail for prayer for themselves and for others. Several requested the laying on of hands for healing. When it came to exchanging the peace, they actually exchanged it. They looked at each other, pressed hands and said, "Peace be with you." How extraordinary! At one point they sang together in the Spirit: a tremulous note struck by someone's voice, others joining in with harmony, a swelling crescendo of cascading notes and tumbling phrases, catching everyone up in an ascending spiral of praise and wonder, and then dying out to a few quivering notes and a silence that could be felt.

The moment for actually breaking the bread and drinking the wine came somehow to everyone's realisation – an exquisite, sensitive moment when they could do no other. For Don, that part was reminiscent of Brethrenism at its very best, and was less new to him than to most of the other 'learners'. When it was all over and they glanced at their watches, they were somehow both surprised and not surprised to discover that three and a half hours had passed without any sense of time, least of all of lagging time.

As Don drove home on the fourth morning he was sure of one thing: whatever might be said of some of its other features the 'new Pentecostalism' knew what it was to worship 'in spirit and in truth' (John 4:24). That was a big point in its favour. For surely a basic test of any authentic Christian movement must be just that. Where worship is pallid, slow, anaemic and uninspiring, the spiritual health of its adherents must be in question. Where it is vital, varied, contemporary, rooted in eternity but expressed with spontaneity, their spiritual health looks good. For man's chief end truly is to glorify God and enjoy him forever.

CHAPTER 10 – IN SPIRIT AND IN TRUTH

Twenty years ago Christian worship in England was in a state of deep crisis. In the Church of England, the only legal forms of service were still couched in the language of the seventeenth century. For all its poetic beauty, its archaic words and style were making it less and less intelligible to all but a diminishing number of lifelong adherents. Among the Evangelicals, determination to stand by the letter of the Prayer book, forged during the ritualistic controversies of the previous hundred years, had stifled change and locked worship into a straightjacket which regarded any innovation, however minor, with the deepest suspicion. Among the Catholics, hard-won freedom to chant in ancient tones of praise, to wear colourful vestments, to mount elaborate processions, to wave incense and to revere the reserved sacrament seemed increasingly irrelevant and anachronistic in fast-emptying churches.

In the Free Churches the situation was little better. Methodist, Baptist, Congregational and Presbyterian worship was largely characterised by the hymn-prayer-reading-sermon-hymn sandwich, itself as archaic as the Anglican forms from which it had once broken free. Brevity was the order of the day. Dangerous indeed was the minister who dared to allow a service to last beyond an hour!

Roman Catholics still used Latin in the central section of the Mass, the eucharistic prayer. Their worship, even more rigid than that in the Church of England, was governed by the canons of the Council of Trent, convened four hundred years before to salvage the church from the ravages of the Reformation.

Even groups like the Plymouth Brethren, which had

bravely pioneered new forms of 'free' worship during the nineteenth century, were finding that their freedom had become stylised with time, and could be as rigid as the set services they so passionately despised.

Across the whole spectrum, English Christians were singing eighteenth – and nineteenth century hymns to equally ancient tunes, reading from the seventeenth-century Bible and praying in an archaic style they would never dream of using outside church. Almost everywhere, worship was led by one or two professionals, while mute and passive congregations watched, listened and only joined as directed in hymns and set responses. No wonder the English church was in decline! Add the dead hand of liberalism and Modernism which had carved up the Bible, denied the supernatural and despised evangelism, and the mixture was complete. A *Guardian* writer could confidently declare "The Christian church in England is in a state of irreversible decline."

Where this sad situation has been reversed in the intervening score and five years, charismatic renewal and worship have almost always been involved. Charismatic Christians have not been afraid to introduce change into forms of worship. But they are not red revolutionaries, seeking change for change's sake and rejecting all that has gone before. Amazingly, they have combined ancient with modern. The Scarborough conference which Don attended may have used a 'new' liturgy for its Communion service, but in fact that liturgy was based on the way the church worshipped in the fourth and fifth centuries, and pre-dated the Prayer Book by over a thousand years. Indeed, charismatic Christians have enthusiastically embraced the new forms of service officially introduced in the Churches of England and Rome. Frequent reference to the Holy Spirit in these services had given charismatic worship that sense of immediacy which Don found so compelling.

In music, too, charismatic Christians have made a dramatic impact. For the first time for a hundred years a whole new genre of song has found its way into Christian worship. Simple songs of adoration, quiet verses of commitment in contemporary musical styles enable Christians to express their faith in modern language they can understand. Yes, some of the new music is shallow and superficial and will not last, but that is true of many secular modern songs. On the other hand, soaring affirmations of the lordship of Christ, assertions of the sufficiency of Jesus the bread of life, and joyful statements of faith in the loving fatherhood of God will find their place in Christian hymnbooks for years to come. Nor have charismatic Christians rejected the classic hymns of yesteryear. Wesley's eighteenth-century masterpieces come alive with fresh power in the Spirit-filled atmosphere of charismatic praise. This combination of ancient and modern marks the movement as authentically Christian. It stands foursquare on the revelation of the Bible and the affirmations of the creeds. Rooted in the past, it is determined to speak convincingly in the present.

Charismatic worship is both formal and spontaneous. Charismatics would insist that that was the initial intention of the earliest Christian liturgies, anyway. They were never designed to be followed word for word, week after week, year after year. Rather, they were suggestions for leaders of churches, defining appropriate structures for different services and suitable ways of praying and leading the worship. That is how they were originally used. Only as the fire of the Spirit burned low did the liturgies become the formal, sterile affairs of later time.

Charismatic worship is led by individuals, but all may take part. In this way the church worships as the body of Christ. "When you come together, each one has a hymn, a lesson, a revelation, a tongue, or an interpretation" (1 Corinthians 14:26). This emphasis on the church as the body of Christ explains why the charismatic movement has made such an impact among Catholics. Ever since the turn of the century, Catholics in the Church of England and in the Church of Rome have been exploring the concept of the body of Christ with particular reference to the Communion service in which every worshipper has his office, or part, to play. Charismatics have come to the same truth from a different direction, and have enriched the work of the earlier liturgical movement.

The fact that renewed worship is spontaneous and shared does not mean that it is disorderly. In our experience the opposite is the case. David was deeply impressed at a conference in Newcastle by the way in which the meetings were controlled from the chair, and possible disorder was nipped in the bud. One night, the ministry of the word was followed by spontaneous worship as one and another prayed, prophesied and sang a familiar song. After a while one song was kept going repetitively. Simple verses additional to the ones printed on the sheet were being made up and the chorus was inserted each time. Eventually, the chairman stepped forward. "Now," he announced, "we'll sing verse three and the chorus just once more and then we'll close the meeting." The verse and chorus were sung and still someone struck up another verse. "No!" called the chairman. "We're going to pronounce the benediction and then do what they did in the early church. We're going out into the world!" And so we did.

Later the same week, the intercessions in the Communion service were thrown open, and anyone in the seven-hundred-strong gathering was invited to lead in prayer. Immediately, one man began to pray in tongues. "No, brother," interrupted the chairman. "There'll be opportunity for the exercise of spiritual gifts later. Now is the time for prayers of intercession." The poor man dissolved in tears, but the meeting was saved.

Many leaders of churches are hesitant about charismatic renewal, fearing their position will be compromised and ordered worship will be reduced to chaos. Well might some of them fear, for when a church enters renewal, qualities of leadership become more important than ever, and sensitivity to the Spirit is vital.

Charismatic worship combines mental and physical expression. Holding hands, raising arms, exchanging hugs, movement and dancing – charismatics do not allow us to leave our bodies at a parking-meter outside the church and come in to worship without them.[1] At the same time, they warn against the fossilising of worship, wherein the emphasis is put on the 'right' actions, the correct place for the Lord's Prayer or the confession, the appropriate phrase, the words that somehow make it all valid.

It is in this area of validity that the charismatic renewal probably has most to say to the church at the end of the twentieth century. For charismatic Christians do not require an episcopally-ordained priest dressed in 'proper' vestments and assuming correct genuflections to make their worship valid, nor is any other kind of properly appointed leader or suitably approved order of service necessary, either. Indeed, charismatics warn that "no organisation, no structuring, no texts, no music, and no ministers will be any use if they do not bring people into touch with God. There is no substitute for encounter with the living God."[2] This makes worship live. Something really happens, because God is present and his people feel him.

At Enon, the regular Sunday worship never became openly charismatic. The traditional Baptist structure remained the norm, though it was often altered for special events, and it regularly throbbed with life. Something similar occurs in very many English 'charismatic' churches of every type – a fact that has disappointed very many of the early pioneers. Christians who have tasted renewal have been asked to respond to a persuasive plea. "Love is the greatest gift and the highest grace. Do not cause your fellow-Christians to stumble by worrying them with radical changes that they find unacceptable. Do not bring discredit on your new experience by pressing it to the point of causing division."

Some have felt this was asking too much. They have walked away and followed leaders with separatist leanings. Others have conformed, with varying degrees of reluctance. They have accepted the fact that they could only be themselves at conferences and special events. That is to their credit. The very least they should receive in recognition is the same treatment as they have given others. How willing are the more traditional Christians to listen to a similar plea? "Do not cause your fellow-Christians to stumble by compelling them to silence the longing of their spirits for freer worship. Do not bring discredit on your beloved tradition by making it an instrument for the quenching of the Spirit."

Perhaps we ourselves were not bold enough. Certainly we were made cautious by sad divisions we saw in other churches. Maybe we were afraid of rocking the boat. Certainly we saw fine church members who knew their Bibles yet were very hesitant indeed about what was happening. Not long before, we had been hesitant, too, until the logic of events made us think again. Perhaps in the end, traditional English reserve won and, to a degree, we ourselves grieved and quenched the Spirit.

Notes

[1] See Colin Buchanan, *Encountering Charismatic Worship*, *(Grove Books,)*
[2] *ibid*.

CHAPTER 11 – MIDNIGHT IN THE RAIN

Another late-night telephone call plunged Don, this time, into the nightmare world of the occult and demon possession. At midnight in the rain, parking in a badly-lit street of Victorian houses, he walked up the path with the message still ringing in his ears. "Don. Can you come at once? This is a nasty one. You'll need the whole armour of God."

Richard had been paying a routine pastoral call at the end of a busy evening. The couple he visited were new members whose recent discovery of Christ had greatly heartened the church. Harry, especially, had a striking story to tell, for his active and enquiring mind had led him down some odd philosophical and psychological avenues before finding the strait gate and the narrow way that leads to life in Christ. He had even dabbled in a little 'black magic', so he admitted before his baptism – some ceremony encouraged by interest in Dennis Wheatley's books. He did not remember the details very clearly by then.

Now Richard was doing his duty as a deacon, and his visit had produced a serious discussion of some Bible topics. Then something eerie had begun to happen. Richard waxed rather eloquent on the authority of the name of Christ and all that the lovely word, 'Jesus', represented in sin covered, death's power broken, and Satan put to shame.

Suddenly Harry jumped to his feet, said, "Wait a minute," and hurried from the room. There were scurrying sounds in the passage, a chair fell over, and Harry reappeared, his face distorted and his hands trembling. Falling to the ground, he literally writhed about, crawled under a table, and then emerged again, shouting incoherently. Efforts to soothe him succeeded for a time, and he sat on a settee, shaken and apologetic. Assuming some kind of emotional breakdown, Richard suggested a quiet prayer and a night's sleep. At the mention of prayer, Harry lost control again and became threatening, abusive and blasphemous. After watching forty minutes of these repeated swings of behaviour, the deacon sent his message to Don.

Knowing nothing of this, Don was let into the house by a scared housewife who led him straight to the large room where the other two sat.

"Don't you start on me! Leave us alone!" yelled Harry, leaping from the chair and pointing at Don as soon as he appeared in the doorway. He ran across the room with grasping hands outstretched.

"In the name of Jesus Christ, *sit down*," commanded Richard, in a clear, cutting voice. Harry stopped in mid-stride, blinked, rubbed his forehead, turned, and took his place on the sofa again.

"I'm terribly sorry, Don." His voice was quiet and recognisable now . . . Harry's voice. "I just can't help it. Something comes over me. Please help me."

The next two hours conjured up the kind of experience of which bad dreams and lurid novels are made. An extraordinary cycle repeated itself every ten or fifteen minutes. Quiet, sane conversation with a Christian alternated with wild outbursts from an apparent madman, mingled with threats, mockery, boasting – "I'll show you my power! Who do you think you are? Tremble before me!" – and occasional attempts at physical violence, always countered with the command to be still, in the name of Jesus.

Don had never been so frightened in his life as he was when, for ten minutes while the tormented man was quiet, Richard left him alone whilst he telephoned several Christian friends to awaken them and get them praying. He could see the next attack coming on visibly, as Harry's fists began to open and close and the wild stare returned to his eyes. Don breathed with relief as Richard chose that moment to return, and stood placidly, his eyes blinking in his broad friendly face, as he was assailed with, "You are the trouble! Leave me alone!"

Clearly they were facing what the Bible describes as

demon-possession. Several times they had said, firmly, "In the name of Jesus Christ, *come out of him*," only to be met, each time, with worse agitation. Then the climax came most unexpectedly. It was a calmer spell. They were taking it in turns to read the Bible very quietly together, not quoting melodramatic passages, but simply sharing psalms that spoke of confidence and refuge in God, and sayings of Jesus which pointed to the care and fatherhood of God. Simply because he preferred to finish a chapter, Richard persevered to the end of Matthew 16, his voice faltering with some dismay as he came to words he had not anticipated. "For what is a man profited, if he shall gain the whole world, and lose his own soul? or what shall a man give in exchange for his soul?" He gazed across at Don, the same realisation visibly dawning on both their faces together.

"That black-magic ceremony you once told me about?" Don whispered.

"Have you ever offered your soul in some kind of exchange?" asked Richard, at the same moment.

"I ca . . . I can't . . . I can't remember," gasped Harry, rising to his feet. The agitation was overcoming him again.

"You must remember a thing like that," they urged.

"I can't tell you . . . I ca . . ." Harry looked around desperately, then fell to his knees and began to shout completely meaningless sounds – no kind of human language – an obscene caricature of speech, in the deep, coarse voice by now so eerily familiar.

"In the name of Jesus Christ, *let him speak*! You cannot stop him. He belongs to Christ. *Let the truth be told*!"

Harry began to crawl on his hands and knees, sobbing. He stopped and squatted, his ravaged and tear-stained face pleading as his normal voice returned. And in quiet, disjointed phrases, the story came out.

He had honestly forgotten the details, had never given them a thought since his conversion, until a few minutes ago. Yes, there had been such a ceremony. He had been promised, 'power to make things happen', in exchange for his soul, offered to the dark forces. As the few words tumbled out his voice rose to a shriek and he thrashed about.

Backed against the wall, they both addressed him . . . it? . . . them? . . . taking turns to speak . . . one speaking whilst the other silently prayed. An extraordinary mixture of feelings affected them both. There was fear, numbing, mouth-drying terror, yet at the same time soaring confidence in the Name which is above every name. They reminded themselves and Harry and whoever or whatever tormented him that the Devil has no right or claims on the one who clings to Jesus. They reversed the stupid and wicked 'bargain' that had been made, and claimed the value of that purchased with Christ's own blood at Calvary, which redeems every Christian. They knew no special formula, exercised no physical restraint, could think of no appropriate ceremonies, had no words to fit except the words of Scripture, and were too scared to shout or gesticulate. Quiet urgent words from dry mouths . . . whispered prayers . . . the patter of rain on leaves and path outside . . . and for Harry, just one more outburst . . . and a sigh, and a face that seemed to expand and then collapse . . . and the battle was over.

Never again was he to be troubled in this way or in any way remotely like it. Certain noticed oddities in his character and demeanour were seen no more. He went on to serve God usefully and quietly for several years, never became a really convinced Baptist, and became increasingly involved in social work of a very Christian nature which took him away from Enon and the district. All of that, of course, was in the future. For the moment, feeling emotionally exhausted and almost physically bruised, they prayed for their respective families and returned to them to find that the same sense of fear had permeated their two homes, but it had lifted.

It was our first unequivocal encounter with spiritual evil personified, and few others were quite so dramatic. We looked for no more encounters; one was enough. But they kept on coming, in one way or another. For we were a church that involved itself in aggressive evangelism, touching people wholly pagan, as so many had become in the Britain of the 1960s. And something very ironical was happening. Among many people who had turned from Christianity (or never met it) and were becoming bored and dissatisfied with empty materialism, there was a wave of interest in the immaterial, the odd, the strange, the inexplicable. Horoscopes were becoming the best-read part of a newspaper. Ouija boards were being sold by a well-known games manufacturer. Spiritualism was on the increase. The watch-maker on the corner of the street seriously told Don he was a white wizard who often talked with the Great Ones of Venus. A bishop recommended seances as interesting evidence of life after death, while a popular Methodist writer quoted the extra-biblical revelations that might be obtained from a medium. The cinema industry was cashing in on a new brand of horror film, very different from the old naïve type which used to make you feel rather sorry for the monster! Eastern religions were making a bid for western attention; some odd forms of 'meditation' were claiming to be purely psychological techniques, but they taught their devotees to chant the names of Hindu spirits.

What was even more ironical was the attitude of exponents of South Bank theology, who were for all their worth persuading the church that the day of the 'religious' and the 'spiritual' was over. Man had come of age; no longer a child, he could not be fed on the mythological concepts of a simpler age, but must be given secular Christianity, religionless Christianity, Christianity without miracles. Faith must abandon the unreal world of spirit and soul, and get out to the real world of politics, education and social service. Prayer must be turned into welfare work, hymns into protest songs, sermons into socio-political dialogue, if there was to be any hope of evangelising (evangelising?) modern, materialistic, secular man.

But at the very moment when trendy, secular theologians were beckoning Christians to advance into the materialistic world to meet the people, hardly anyone was noticing that the people were streaming past them in the other direction, away from materialism into experience, anything that produced an inner happening – mind-enlarging drugs, Satanic ceremonies, upturned glasses, tarot cards and new religious cults.

The harvest was not slow in coming. Ministers, evangelists, youth-leaders found themselves responding to cries for help from people who had waded over their ears into something they did not understand, and who found that not many church leaders understood the supernatural, either.

Many came to us through Christian doctors and a Christian psychiatrist. Because they were around, it was possible to keep to a general rule that we would only tackle the para-normal or supernatural in the presence and with the advice of someone medically qualified. Clearly we were treading in a minefield, and we had to learn to distinguish between areas of the psychosomatic, the mentally disturbed, the hydra-headed monster of depression, the hysterical, and so on.

Often there was an overlap. Someone inclined to depression might well become entangled with psychedelic drugs. A neurotic personality might find a sleazy cult attractive. An obsessive gambler might dabble in the occult to increase his betting chances. A deep sense of rejection, drug or alcohol addiction, black magic or spiritualism often seem to go hand in hand. The area of harm done by each overlaps, and the rejection complex can remain when the other problems have been dealt with. Drugs, sexual deviation and the occult also often go together; the third is at first simply a source of supply for the other two, but it takes over and becomes an independent power in itself. Preoccupation with mild eccentricities like yoga, fortune-telling and star-casting often appeals to rootless personalities who drift from one novelty to another, yet despise the black-and-white standards of the Bible, airily dismissing them as less than spiritual.

A doctor asked us to help with a persistently haunted house. A married couple and two children were troubled with mysteriously-slammed doors, shaking windows, creaking boards, bad dreams and shadowy movements just seen out of the corner of the eye. There was reason to suspect (though no certainty) that a medium had died in the house. We prayed in each room (and cupboard!) that the sanctifying power of Christ would drive out any bad influences. In the final room, as we prayed, we heard a crash downstairs and a cry. A kitchen window had flung open and one of the children had fainted. It was the end of any mysterious happenings. Poltergeists? Adolescent emotions somehow channelled physically? Perhaps. At any rate, the name of Jesus brought peace.

A young wife was terrified by constantly-recurring nightmares which were always the same. She was a little girl again, standing outside a room which she recognised from her childhood. She was being drawn inside, frightened and struggling, by an invisible power. Enquiries elicited the fact that her mother had gone through a spell of dabbling in spiritualism in that room during the daughter's childhood. A simple prayer with reading of the Scriptures – "There is no fear in love, but perfect love casts out fear" (1 John 4:18) – "Lord, this young woman belongs to you. Jesus Christ is her Saviour. Fear and darkness are no part of the inheritance of a child of God. In the name of Jesus, we go out against this fear and dismiss it. Amen." The nightmare never came again.

CHAPTER 12 – NO OTHER NAME

Witchcraft, poltergeists, spiritualism: once we were aware of them, there was much evidence linking demonism also with the off-beat anti-church cults of the semi-Christian lunatic fringe. As a result of a doorstep call, David spent several months during this period studying the literature of one group with international headquarters in New York. He finally came to the reluctant conclusion that demonic activity was the only explanation for the bizarre and bewildering mixture of truth and falsehood which he found in their books. He discovered something else, too. The sect claimed to be utterly faithful to the teaching of the Bible. That claim was maintained all through the first book, the second book and the first four hundred and fifty pages of the third book he studied. Then something else began to happen, something which a disciple of the movement, carefully schooled in the question-and-answer method of group discussion, would never have noticed. A new phrase made its appearance with increasing frequency.

"First in 1920 *did we discern*" David read, "that the good news of God's kingdom as *established* in the heavens in 1914 (A.D.) was to be preached in fulfilment of Matthew 24:14."[1] How did they discern? No answer was supplied. Later he read, "in 1935 . . . *it was disclosed* . . ."[2] Later still: "The stricken condition of such 'men' . . . *was revealed* . . ."[3] And later still: "It was not till the *Watch Tower* magazine's issue of July 15, 1925, that Jehovah's modern Christian witnesses *got the understanding* that this final war (of Armageddon) would be . . . a universal war . . . *This information has since been expanded and enlarged upon Scripturally*.[4] The truth at last! The sect did not teach or proclaim the Bible. It taught its own brand of doctrine, specially revealed, and made the Bible fit. Later still

David's book asserted that man's final salvation was to be found, not in the Bible, but in further additions to it yet to be published during the millenium.[5]

This 'extra' to scripture, necessary to salvation, is a common element in all the semi-Christian, exclusive cults – *The Book of Mormon, Revelations of Mary Baker Eddy, Prophecies of Mrs White, The Angel Moroni*, and so on. Always something added to the Bible, the Something Else from Someone Out There. It is the essence of the occult experience. It falls under the warning addressed to Israel: "When they say to you, 'Consult the mediums and the wizards who chirp and mutter,' should not a people consult their God? Should they consult the dead on behalf of the living? To the teaching and the testimony! Surely for this word which they speak there is no dawn" (Isaiah 8:19,20). It conforms to the judgment of the apostles that demons and false spirits are the source of anti-Christian teaching, especially the kind that claims to be Christian (see 1 Timothy 4:1, 1 John 4:1-3). What else but demons could persuade intelligent people to believe the palpable nonsense associated with some of these groups – gold plates dug up which then disappear, magic spectacles with which to read them, which in turn disappear, and so on.

We learned a great deal about another American group at its deeper levels from a young woman who fled to us for protection. Insecure and deprived, but very intelligent, she had drifted into the sect and had become a committed disciple. Ceremonies of a clearly occult nature had followed in a 'temple'. She was 'spiritually married' to one of the officers, and discovered that a 'spiritual husband' has sexual rights over his 'wives', and something less definable and more sinister, too. For when she took fright and left the movement (going on to heroin addiction as a result – the same pattern again) she discovered that her 'husband' could 'call her back'. She saw a vision of him, and felt an overwhelming compulsion to return. Later, converted to Christ through the witness of a Pentecostal pastor, she was delivered from drug-addiction, but still oppressed and haunted by this 'calling'. Persistent and repeated rejection of the influence in the name of Jesus Christ eventually won the day, but only after a wearying struggle.

A similar experience several years later showed the same kind of phenomenon with yet another American-based group. A charming and personable young man was infiltrating the church's youth fellowship. All was honey and soft words as he chatted with Don over a cup of coffee, while lovingly fingering a Bible. His church taught that Jesus Christ was a failure? Wherever did Don get that idea? They made their leader superior to Christ? Never! They questioned the authority of Scripture? How could that be so, since they constantly quoted it! Don grew bored with this fencing with words, and applied a different test. The forces of evil simply cannot bear direct reference to the name which above every name, at which 'every knee shall bow', in heaven and on earth and under the earth, and 'every tongue confess that Jesus Christ is Lord, to the glory of God the Father (see Philippians 2:9-11). Don looked the young man in the eyes and quoted this. He immediately became agitated. The gloves were off and there was direct confrontation. His temper rapidly broke as Don smilingly and quietly quoted again, 'Every knee shall bow.'

"Bow! Jesus Christ has already bowed to our Leader!" he shouted. "You know nothing of these things, with your stupid Bible quotations! Spirit beings often visit *me* and bring *me* revelations. Jesus Christ does too! I often visit him! You ministers of false churches! When did *you* ever visit Christ?"

"I don't have to visit him, I abide in him," Don smilingly replied. "He is my Lord, and Lord of all."

The young man stormed to the door. "Well, we know where we stand with each other! You are my enemy in this town, and I'll fight you with everything I have! You'll find what real power is!"

Don and the church mobilised intense prayer for the young man, or rather against him, and he met with almost complete failure, looking more and more tired and harassed until he left the area.

Another adolescent, disturbed and unhappy, came

under an almost hypnotic influence, learning the tenets and phraseology of the same group in an astonishingly short time, and turning abusively against his former Christian friends. When reminded of the authority of the name of Jesus he became hysterical, claiming that he wanted to abandon his new religion, but "they won't let me. They haunt me. If I talk about them, they'll make me go mad." Further Bible-reading and quiet reassurance in prayer seemed to break whatever strange influence was troubling him.

This is not, of course, to suggest that all members of semi-Christian cults are demon-possessed. Many of them are genuine, sincere folk even if, in our view, they are deceived and deluded. But we do assert that demonic activity lies behind the movements. Their addition of special revelation to the teaching of the Bible and their frequent exaltation of someone above Jesus Christ himself is evidence of their fundamental rejection of Christ and their aggressive anti-Christian character.[6]

If, however, it was in Sunderland that we first began to understand the demonic forces underlying the sub-Christian cults, it was in the area of the ouija board that their power was most chillingly displayed. Ted was a thick-set, bull-necked, working man with ginger hair, snub-nose and freckles. He was subject to depression, which kept him from employment for quite long periods. He was also a compulsive gambler, and began to use the board to obtain racing tips. Several of his family – sisters, cousins and others – were interested in spiritualism and used their boards for semi-religious purposes. From his board, Ted began receiving tips, allegedly from the spirit of his deceased mother. For a time they were good tips. Then they began to be nonsense. But his mother's 'voice' could now be heard, 'inside his head', more and more frequently, and whether or not he welcomed it. Now he was beginning to have an obsessive feeling that if he killed his wife, his problems would somehow be solved. Scared and ashamed, he poured out his troubles to his doctor. He in turn asked him if he would be prepared to welcome a Baptist minister into his home. Don was on his way, now, by appointment.

Richard was out of town that morning, which made Don uneasy. He collected Peter, another of the deacons, and tried to prime him as they drove across town. "This may be demon possession, and there may be some kind of confrontation," he explained. "If that happens whenever I'm talking, you keep silently praying. If you need to speak, I'll start praying!"

"Right-ho," replied Peter rather dubiously. He confessed later that his thoughts were, "Gosh! Don does dramatise things. We'll do a bit of listening, give some advice, say a prayer and arrange to meet again. That's all."

Ted lived in a typical terrace of little back-to-back houses in a rundown working-class area of Sunderland. Don and Peter were shown into the 'best room' reserved for special occasions, and looking rather unlived-in. But there was a surprise in store. Ted had called together his interested relatives – sisters, brother-in-law, mother-in-law, nephew and niece. They sat in upright chairs around the walls, waiting to see what would happen. It was like the apostle Peter's visit to Cornelius at Caesarea, Don reflected ruefully, though the outcome was hardly likely to be so happy.

Making the best of it, for there was no inclination to notice his hint that perhaps this was a private matter, Don asked Ted to tell his story. It came out in a fumbling manner; he was a rough, simple fellow, a manual worker, little educated and not very good at communicating, but the details were very much as the doctor had described. He was particularly sure about his mother's messages. At first they had come through the ouija board. Now they came directly. "I sort of hear her voice inside my head, without really hearing it," he tried to explain. "Matter of fact, she's talking now," he added eerily.

"What is she saying?" Don's lips were dry.

"Well, she says I'm not to listen to you. She says you deceive people and I haven't to take your advice."

There was a stirring amongst the relatives, then a short

90

silence that seemed very long. Don tried not to lick his lips, and to keep a tremble out of his voice. "Ted, that is not your mother speaking to you. Do you really think that your *mother* would encourage you to gamble, knowing the harm it does you?" The doctor had told Don that. "Do you suppose your *mother* would tell you to attack your wife? Would she call a church minister a deceiver?"

Ted looked puzzled, rasping his thumb and forefinger over his stubbly chin. Don looked him in the eyes, and with a rapid, silent prayer and a signal to Peter to pray like mad, he addressed what lay behind that 'voice'. "You are not Ted's mother. You are a lying and deceiving spirit. I command you in the name of the Lord Jesus Christ to be silent, and to stop your lies."

The reaction was the opposite to what Don hoped for. With a bellow, Ted jumped to his feet, his limbs quivering. In a gravelly voice, something like his own, but more coarse, he poured out threats and curses, indecencies and blasphemies. This lasted for ten minutes non-stop, and if it did nothing else, it made it abundantly clear that Ted's mother had nothing to do with it. It was the beginning of the most horrifying five hours Don has ever spent. The details have never clarified in his memory. There were certainly several physical attacks on himself and Peter, each stopped by further invoking of the name of Jesus. There were capering obscenities and attempts at exposure. There were chilling blasphemies of a theological finesse quite beyond anyone who did not understand theology. There was a good deal of boasting about 'showing you our power'; Don noticed the plural with sinking heart. Ted threatened them both, using their Christian names which they had never mentioned, having introduced themselves as 'Reverend Bridge and Mr Watson'. Most chilling of all (and Don has come across the same thing years later in a different part of the country), when they referred to Jesus as the Lord and the One to whom every knee must finally bow, the voice actually said, "He's not! He's not! He's dead! I saw him die! I was there!"

"Then you know that he rose again," Don replied, more

calmly than he felt. "That demonstrates that he is Lord, and all power is his."

"Power! What do you know of power? This can go on forever. You're losing, you know it!" the voice jeered back. So the battle went on. At one stage they withdrew to fetch Richard, who would, they knew, be home by now. Ted's jeering laughter followed them. But when they returned half-an-hour later he was subdued, tearful, apologetic. Quiet talk, Bible reading and prayer were occasionally interrupted by more outbursts, including one in which Ted snapped and bit at Richard's hand raised in prayer. Eventually, eleven demons came out.

The end of the story was less than successful. Working closely with doctor and psychiatrist, both committed Christians with no doubts whatever about the real, objective existence of demons, Ted was nursed through a long course of quiet counselling, frequent prayer, the encouraging of sensible habits, the acceptance of Christian instruction, attendance at public worship. There were no more outbursts and he turned very willingly away from the ouija board. But the 'voice' persisted, less dominant, more resistible, but still there, a more than occasional background to his life; there was no pretence of his mother now, but open evil, yet coaxing. And about gambling, Ted was very, very stubborn. Since this had been the opening for the evil influence to exploit, he was urged to renounce it as firmly as he had renounced the influence itself. But he would not. He would not even try, or pray for help in that respect. It remained an area wide open to attack again, and Ted became a shadowy and rather pathetic figure on the outskirts of church life, but never really committed.

Not so the astonished relatives who had witnessed all this in the house. It was not so very different from the household of Cornelius, after all. As one, they burned their ouija-boards and turned up in church the following Sunday. At their insistence, Don visited the home weekly to give systematic Bible instruction. At the end of the course, five of them asked for baptism and church membership. When the time came for Don to leave Sunderland, they were among the most affectionate and tearful, and clubbed together for a special personal gift in addition to the presentation made by the church.

Notes

[1] *'Babylon the Great Has Fallen!' God's Kingdom Rules!* (Watchtower Bible and Tract Society of New York, Inc., 1963), 463 (italics ours).

[2] *ibid.*, 516, (italics ours).

[3] *ibid.*, 532, (italics ours).

[4] *ibid.*, 563, (italics ours).

[5] *ibid.*, 646, (italics ours).

[6] See Michael Green, *I Believe in Satan's Downfall* (Hodder & Stoughton, 1981), ch.6, for a fuller treatment of demonic influence in counterfeit religion.

CHAPTER 13 – THE DEMONS BELIEVE[1]

Devils? Demons? Evil spirits? Charismatic Christians' insistence on the reality of Satan and all his host threatens, in the eyes of some, to take the church back into the Middle Ages, not forward into the twenty-first century. "They'll be hunting and drowning witches next!" they fear. "Surely," they reason, "scientific understanding has delivered mankind once and for all from the fear and superstition associated with literal belief in a personal devil who controls malign, unseen forces." But has it? Is it any more unreasonable to believe in a personal devil who is evil than in a loving God who is good? A glance at the world scene suggests as much evidence for the one as for the other.

The very survival of humanity is today in doubt. The nuclear arms race threatens destruction on an unimaginable scale. Mindless exploitation of the earth's natural resources makes mankind's continuing ability to maintain and supply itself unlikely. The widening gap between rich and poor threatens global war in one last desperate bid to seize what remains. Sweeping movements of human thought capture the minds of millions. They offer drastic 'solutions' as macabre as the holocaust of the Jews and the racial murder of Cambodia. Even political commentators sometimes liken the irrational behaviour of some of the world's leaders to the headlong rush of the Gadarene swine.[2] But who started that rush? Demons, according to the Bible! James Stewart observes, "When men and nations of decent average morality are caught up and involved in such a situation, driven by an almost irresistible compulsion – who can doubt that something living and demonic is at work?"[3]

Nor is it necessarily unscientific to believe in a personal devil. The atheist, of course, rejects God as well, but then

94

he is left with a problem. If the universe is one gigantic accident, man himself and man's mind are part of that accident. Why then, should men's thoughts and ideas have any value? Belief in God, on the other hand, in a loving, personal, rational intelligence who creates and sustains the universe, gives it a rational ground and moral purpose. And the presence of evil in the world then necessitates belief in a personal devil, as well. For if God alone is finally responsible for everything that happens, he must be a fiendish being of monstrous proportions to countenance and tolerate the evil that exists within it. To be sure, God and the devil cannot be equals, locked from eternity in struggle for victory, for that would make the devil another god. there will always be mystery behind God's goodness, his power, and the problem of evil. But God is not the author of sin, and it is therefore hard to resist the conclusion that a personal devil is present in the world, actively opposed to God's loving purpose and care.

Belief in God also demands belief in a spiritual dimension. In that dimension, the Bible says, angels live along with God. Some of them are good. Others are bad. The Bible calls them demons. Like men in the physical world, they are fallen. They have become the agents of Satan, the Devil himself. As C. S. Lewis points out, "This seems to me to explain a good many facts. It agrees with the plain sense of Scripture, the tradition of Christendom, and the beliefs of most men at most times. And it conflicts with nothing that any of the sciences has shown to be true."[4]

Around the turn of the present century the Austrian pioneer Sigmund Freud described mental illness in the now familiar categories of complexes, psychoses, neuroses and so on. He added the theory that all such disorders can be traced back to repressed sexual development in infancy. As a result, he and his followers, considered they had explained away the Bible's insistence that some mental disorders can be caused by demon possession.

Freud's views, however, have not always been followed. One of his most outstanding students, Carl Gustav Jung, came to the quite different conclusion that disorders in the subconscious mind can have an independent existence of their own. "They can take over the control of the total personality – to such a degree that the free will is suspended. No, the demons are not banished."[5] He drew evidence for this not only from individual patients, but also from the whole Nazi movement. He warned that the defeat of Germany in the Second World War would not eradicate it: "The victorious nations can just as suddenly become a victim of the demonic powers."[6] How right he was!

For the Christian, of course, the witness of the Bible is crucial in settling the issue of Satan's existence. That witness is quite clear. Satan is particuarly present at the beginning, in the middle and at the end of the Bible story – that is, at creation, at the cross and in the last day. The Bible announces his defeat and ultimate destruction. Attempts to explain this away as the language of symbolism are unconvincing. Symbols of what? To speak of human weakness, wickedness and folly in the language of demons is badly misleading, unless they exist. Other language, like 'sickness', 'lostness' and 'darkness' is much more appropriate. In fact, this is exactly how the Bible speaks when it does describe the human condition rather than Satan's activity.

The Bible's witness to Satan's reality comes into sharpest focus in its accounts of the life and teaching of Jesus. Jesus confronted possessed men and women (the literal translation is *demonised*). He exercised total authority over evil powers and expelled them. He distinguished between physical sickness, mental illness and demonism, and was careful to show that they were not all the same thing (see Matthew 4:24). He described his own death and resurrection as a conflict with the prince of darkness and a breaking of his power (see Luke 22:53 and John 12:31). Was he mistaken? Was he merely accommodating his language to the popular thought-forms of his day? The Christian believes that Jesus is Lord and that he is truth. This should settle the issue.

Not that the Bible blames all sickness, mental distress and human misbehaviour on the direct activity of demons. Some in the charismatic movement have gone far beyond

Scripture in seeing demons at every turn. They have brought disrepute on themselves and sorrow to their hearers. Normally, if a man is bad-tempered he does not need a 'spirit of temper' (*sic*) cast out of him. He needs to read his Bible and say his prayers and put on the mind of Christ in gentleness and patience. The best treatment for a man who drinks too much will rarely be exorcism. He needs to give heed to the apostolic command, "Do not get drunk with wine, for that is debauchery; but be filled with the Spirit" (Ephesians 5:18). The normal treatment for jealousy is not to cast out a 'spirit of envy' (?) but to see oneself by faith as a child of God, accepted unreservedly by grace, with no need to be insecure or to adopt someone else's image.

The Bible's testimony is that those who are truly demon-possessed declare themselves when confronted with the person of Jesus or with his Spirit-filled followers. That was our experience in Sunderland, and it has proved to be the same ever since. Christians need never go looking for those who are possessed; when God is ready he will bring them their way.

Nor will deliverance always be the right response. Some are hardened in their possession and happy with it. Any attempt at exorcism will be throwing pearls before swine (see Matthew 7:6). Sometimes God gives Christians a brush with demons, just to remind them of their existence and the spiritual forces with which they are at war. David was troubled by a boy at the school where he teaches. Every time they passed in the corridor the boy cracked filthy, obscene jokes about Jesus and the crucifixion, and accompanied them with wild, cackling laughter. Like Ted's utterances in the last chapter, some of the jokes displayed rare theological understanding. David began to feel like Paul at Philippi, who was followed for many days by the girl with the spirit of divination (see Acts 16:16-18). He began to wonder if, just for the sake of the other youngsters who always overheard the jokes, he should rebuke and silence the boy in the name of Jesus. But, surprisingly, the corridor confrontations ceased as suddenly as they had begun, and the crisis passed.

Nor will deliverance always be 'successful'. Jesus describes the unclean spirit which wanders through waterless places, seeking rest after going out of a man. Eventually, it returns with seven other spirits and the last state of that man is worse than the first (see Matthew 12:43-45; Luke 11:24-26). The words are generally understood to refer to those who are delivered and then fail to repent of their sins and take Jesus as Lord. They provide ready entrance for the spirits when they return. Perhaps that was why Ted was never really delivered. He would not renounce the gambling which had led him into the occult in the first place.

Some of the most tragic stories to come out of the charismatic renewal have concerned attempted exorcisms that have failed. In two notorious cases which have come to court, murder has been involved. They serve as a severe warning to all who would exercise a deliverance ministry. The gift of distinguishing between spirits is vital (see 1 Corinthians 12:10). The utmost care and wisdom are necessary at every stage in the process.

In *But Deliver us from Evil* John Richards has wisely advised several sessions to deliver those possessed by many demons. At the end of each session the spirits are bound in the name of Jesus, and then released at the beginning of the next. During the sessions the spirits are required to identify themselves one by one, together with the occasion and circumstances of their possession. One by one they are then called out.[2] Perhaps if that advice had been available to Don, Peter and Richard in their confrontation with Ted, there might have been a happier outcome.

The Bible speaks of evil spirits, of fallen angels, of demons, of principalities and powers. It attributes to intelligent and malign spirits some of the obsessions, perversions and psychoses which Jung himself admits, "have a sort of ego . . . a fragmentary personality."[3] No fact of modern science denies this possibility. The control-centres of human life can be dominated by a number of powers independent of the human will. Alcohol, brain-washing, psychedelic drugs, sexual perversion and mental sickness can all do it. The Bible says that evil spirits can do it, too.

Nothing in science has disproved this assertion: much in contemporary Christian experience supports it.

But the power of evil spirits, though great, is limited. Satan, their master, is a defeated foe. Now, "the demons believe – and shudder" (James 2:19). The Christian is called to "put on the whole armour of God, that you may be able to stand against the wiles of the devil" (Ephesians 6:11). He is encouraged to "resist the devil and he will flee from you" (James 4:7). This 'roaring lion' is not to be taken lightly, nor are his allies (see 1 Peter 5:8). "The Lord rebuke you," is the right language to use for the authority is not ours: it is the Lord's (See Jude 9). He has won a resounding victory and struck a swingeing blow against Satan and all his hosts, disarming them, making a public example of them, and triumphing over them at the cross (see Colossians 2:15 and note). Now Jesus reigns, seated at his Father's right hand, till all his enemies are made a stool for his feet (see Hebrews 1:13). To him be the glory, for ever and ever. Amen.

Notes

[1]For much of our argument in the early part of this chapter we are deeply indebted to Michael Green, *I Believe in Satan's Downfall*, pp. 18-29. We warmly commend the entire book to all who are concerned with the reality of Satan's existence, and to all who are in any way involved in deliverance ministry.

[2]See Mark 5:1-20.

[3]James S. Stewart, *A Faith to Proclaim* (Hodder & Stoughton, 1953), 89.

[4]C. S. Lewis, *The Screwtape Letters*, Collins, preface to Fontana edition, 1961.

[5]Quoted in J. A. E. Vermaat, *Jung and the Supernatural, Third Way* (June 1980).

[6]*ibid*.

CHAPTER 14 – THE SCARLET WOMAN?

The wings of the Newcastle to Belfast plane dipped and banked, circling above bright green fields and a lough sparkling in the sunshine beneath the frowning hills of Tyrone. Don was on his way to conduct a ten-day teaching ministry among a group of Baptist communities on the Ards Peninsula. He had jumped at the invitation from a minister-friend, for Ulster was suddenly in the news. A Civil Rights Movement was mounting mass protest marches. A strident-voiced girl-MP was attracting television cameras wherever she went. A gravel-throated, bull-necked, self-ordained cleric of the opposite persuasion was juggling with a large church, a new denomination, the Stormont Parliament and the House of Commons, all at the same time. There was dark talk of civil war, the IRA, 'selling down the river', and the return of the 'killing times'. Catholics claimed they were kept from jobs and housing; Protestants warned that Catholics planned to out-breed them in twenty years' time and then hand them over to the South. The year was 1968.

Don found the Irish Baptists delightful people – humble, friendly, Bible-loving, honest and hard-working. In evangelistic zeal and effectiveness they were second to none. In two years the group Don visited had planted new, thriving, growing churches in three neighbouring villages; in the late sixties few Baptist churches in England could have matched that. Every evening when the services were finished, in one home or another Don was regaled with strong tea, platefuls of freshly-baked scones, and long conversations far into the night. The talk was sometimes serious, sometimes light-hearted fun, but over all hung the deep, dark shadow of religious suspicion and prejudice.

"Should I wear a clerical collar?" Don asked, one night.

"A *Roman* collar? Dear me, no!" came the shocked reply.

"What do I do if I meet a Catholic priest in the village street?" Don pressed. "In England I would expect to pass the time of day with him as a fellow-professional."

"If you do, you may as well catch the next plane home," came an equally shocked response.

Don was careful not to mention Oliver Cromwell, one of his own private heroes but a monster-figure in Ireland because of the massacre of Drogheda and Wexford in the seventeenth century. When he finally voiced his caution, his friends laughed. "No problem with Cromwell – he only killed *Catholics*!" they explained.

A brief visit to Belfast painted in the background more clearly: the grim and ill-named Unity Flats, the semi-slums of the Falls Road, the twenty-foot slogans on house ends: Paisley, IRA Rules, Kick the Pope, No Surrender, England Out! Eighteen months later the Ulster scene erupted into violence. Riots rocked the streets. Blood was shed. Terror, violence, intimidation, bullets and petrol-bombs became part of everyday life for hundreds and thousands of ordinary, innocent folk. Bombay Street, straddled between Catholic Falls and Protestant Shankill, burned from end to end. Six thousand British troops landed in the Province. Part of the United Kingdom had, it seemed, gone mad.

What is this Catholic/Protestant prejudice, and why has it torn the heart of the Western church for the past four hundred years? In Ireland it is part of a compound of a thousand years of imperial conquest, political treachery, economic exploitation and colonial expansion by hated English and Protestant Scots. But it is part of British history, too, and the suspicions remain, even if the currents run more deeply and more quietly. Children still sing:

> Mary, Mary, quite contrary,
> How does your garden grow?
> With silver bells and cockleshells,
> And pretty maids all in a row!

Contrary Mary was Catholic Queen of Scots. She rang the silver bell at Mass and plotted to seize the English throne from Protestant Elizabeth I. She scandalised John Knox and Reformed opinion in Scotland with a series of adulterous and murderous affairs. A dress with cockleshell design, given by her first husband, the Dauphin of France, symbolised the depths of her depravity. Through all her tortuous adventures she was aided and abetted by her ladies-in-waiting, the pretty maids all in a row. Few today may know the meaning of the rhyme or care if they do, but subconscious race memories are transmitted from one generation to another four hundred years after the events which gave them birth.

In English schools pupils are still taught of Catholic opposition to Wycliffe's Bible; of the horrors of the Spanish Inquisition; of Latimer's human torch lighting a candle that would never be put out; of God's miraculous (*sic*) destruction of the Spanish Armada on the storm-tossed rocky shores of Scotland and Ireland; of Bonnie Prince Charlie's ill-starred invasion; of Catholic treachery in Ireland constantly uniting with England's enemies in time of war. On and on, an endless cacophony of bitterness and hatred continues to fill the national mind, even if television now fulfils man's natural need for vicarious cruelty. So when Don's father, in his unregenerate youth, mixed ink with the holy water in a Catholic church so that the worshippers sprinkled their faces blue, he was being no more than a true-blooded, patriotic Englishman. Fifty years later, most English children still do not think of Catholics as Christians.

Because we were reared in godly, evangelical homes we both had extra fuel added to the flames of national prejudice received at school. Our parents were Protestants and proud of it. They read the Bible and obeyed it. They prayed to God and not to saints. They confessed their sins to Jesus, needing no human intermediary, like the Catholics with their priests. Indeed, all Christians were priests (1 Peter 2:9), so that special men in special clothes with special powers were totally unnecessary. Jesus and Jesus alone was

102

to be worshipped and adored rather than the Virgin Mary whom the wicked Catholics had exalted above Christ.

David's grandmother always spoke of Catholics with a shudder. Don learned they were feckless, needlessly poor with irresponsibly large families, Irish by descent and ridden with Irish priests and nuns. Once, David's mother took him round St Marie's Church in Sheffield (now St Marie's Cathedral), pointing out the statues of Mary, the incense burning above the high altar, the strange confession-boxes like divided wardrobes with little grills through which the priest muttered indescribable blasphemies and called them the forgiveness of sins. It was all so different from their own stark, simple mission hall where Christ was worshipped in purity and truth. Visiting preachers sometimes declared that the scarlet woman whose destruction is foretold in Revelation 17 and 18 was none other than the Church of Rome, the Antichrist that even now had come into the world.

Nor had Catholic opposition to Protestants changed, either. During the nineteen fifties it was a matter of plain fact that evangelical believers in Colombia, supported by Don's church, were arrested by Catholic police and forced to eat human excrement and drink human urine. Two of Don's personal friends (missionaries in Brazil) lost their baby when the local priest forbade the captain of the Amazon steamer to take mother and child to hospital when illness struck. When Don himself became an open-air preacher in England he was physically assaulted by Catholics, not for attacking their religion, for he never did, but for preaching the free grace of God.

Doctrinal disagreement still lay at the heart of the Catholic/Protestant divide. Protestants stood for Scripture alone, faith alone and grace alone. Catholics added tradition to Scripture, religious works to faith, and deserts to grace; Protestants and Catholics cordially agreed that this was so. Catholics believed that the bread and wine in the Mass underwent a physical change and became the actual body and blood of Christ, by means of a miracle performed only by a priest who had power over God to call him down on the altar. Don was repeatedly told this by Catholic laymen and by open-air preachers of the Catholic Truth Society. If he was mistaken in thinking this was what Catholics really believed, then so were they.

Now and again, just occasionally, our complacency was stirred. Little things jolted our black-and-white understanding of history and Christian truth. On country walks in the Peak District, David often passed the grey-stoned walls of Padley Chapel. There, in 1588, two Roman Catholic priests had been arrested, taken to Derby and hanged, drawn and quartered for their faith. Fancy Protestants doing that! Only Catholics did that to Protestants, David thought. Ah, well, they were Catholics, and no doubt deserved their fate! He hurried on to enjoy the natural beauty of the Derwent valley.

Then there was that hymn:

> Jesus, the very thought of Thee
> With sweetness fills my breast;
> But sweeter far Thy face to see,
> And in thy presence rest.

Bernard of Clairvaux, a Catholic monk, had written that in the twelfth century, four hundred years before the light of Reformation had dawned. How odd! How strange!

Little did we know, in those faraway days, that God was beginning to prepare our hearts for change, change in attitudes and understanding. And when the change came, once again it was charismatic renewal which provided the catalyst, and taught us that the God of all grace makes all things new.

CHAPTER 15 – THEIR FATHER IS YOURS

One Saturday night, soon after we went to Sunderland, we appeared together on television. The local commercial company ran a weekly programme in which they interviewed a guest celebrity and then held a studio discussion with a panel of four experts and a larger group of local folk. For once, they had decided to 'do religion'. They figured that the charismatic movement might stir a little passing interest among the millions of apathetic viewers at whom their show was directed. The actress, Dora Bryan gave a moving account of her recent conversion to Christ; we joined in the discussion afterwards. One member of the 'experts' panel was the Roman Catholic Bishop of Newcastle who spoke encouragingly of renewal among Catholics, particularly in the United States. For the first time in our lives we commended Christ to the multitudes *with* a Catholic rather than *against* him. Afterwards, we could hardly believe what had happened.

Then Don went to Scarborough and met the Catholic layman who asked if Methodists believe in the deity of Christ. The trouble is, some of them don't. Nor do some Anglicans and Baptists. Talking to him at some length one afternoon as they strolled in the garden, Don had a queer sense of the earth tipping slightly on its axis. For a few odd moments he began to "see ourselves as others see us", or rather, to see Protestants through Catholic eyes. Protestants, at some time or other, have denied as many biblical truths, fallen into as many moral corruptions, and killed as many reglious martyrs as have the Catholics.

"Of course, there is a difference," Don hurriedly told himself. "Because we have the Bible as our ultimate authority, the Holy Spirit keeps recalling us to the truth, and revival comes." But that was precisely what his companion

105

was saying had happened to him, and to lots of his Catholic heroes in the past – Francis of Assisi, Bernard of Clairvaux, Martin Luther . . .

"Martin Luther? Hold on a minute . . ."

"But don't you agree," Don's new friend asked smoothly, "that the Reformation was the clash between Augustine's doctrine of salvation and Augustine's doctrine of the church?"

Don escaped as soon as possible, and later nobbled the organiser of the conference, a cheerful Anglican with an impeccable evangelical pedigree. "You talk about Catholics being filled with the Spirit," Don pressed. "When it happens, does it make them more evangelical?"

"Not always," he replied. "But it makes them more like Christ."

That was a bit below the belt, really, because he knew very well what Don meant. He did not mean evangelical in a party sense, but as descriptive of a way of life which faithfully reflects the New Testament itself. When Catholics are 'baptised in the Spirit', do they take the authority of Scripture more seriously? Do they drop traditional practices which conflict with Scripture? Do they stop preaching salvation-by-sacrament and start preaching salvation-by-faith?

"Look Don, the Holy Spirit is the Spirit of truth," stressed one of the Enon deacons on his return. "You know that. You've said it from your own pulpit a hundred times. He has promised to lead us into all truth. He has inspired the Bible and completed it with the end of the New Testament. Holy Spirit cannot contradict Holy Spirit. What he does and says in the church today cannot contradict what he does and says in the New Testament. Are these folk going to stop praying to Mary? Are they going to start preaching the gospel? Are they going to admit there is one mediator between God and man, the man Christ Jesus?"

Don could hardly complain. His whole ministry was designed to produce Christians who would think biblically. He agreed with everything the deacon said. If something was going on in Rome . . . well, he could fall back on the words of the patron saint of temporary sitters-on-the-fence, good old Gamaliel. "If this plan or undertaking is of men, it will fail; but if it is of God, you will not be able to overthrow them" (Acts 5:38,39). But that could only provide a temporary solution.

For quite separate reasons, we left Sunderland within three months of each other in the summer of 1972. Don went to Frinton in Essex, David to Derby in the Midlands. To his utter surprise, David joined his parish church, and within five years was training for the ministry at Lincoln Theological College. Not only did this bring him into contact with Anglican Catholics but also he was soon grappling with the mystery of transubstantiation.

"Go and read Aquinas for yourself," suggested an understanding tutor one day. 'You'll find him beautiful to read, amazingly simple and lucid, wonderfully humble and gracious."

Aquinas! Dare David read Aquinas? That arch-heretic! That idolater! That deceiver of the church who had taught Christians to worship a piece of bread, believing it to be the actual crucified body of Jesus himself! Dare David read him?

With trembling hands he found the modern sixty-volume American translation of the *Summa Theologiae* on the library shelves, selected the appropriate material on the eucharist and began to read. "Christ is not then by bodily presence in the sacrament of the altar,"[1] he read to his astonishment. Nor was the eucharist a repetition of the sacrifice of Christ, as David had always been taught that Catholics believed.

Is Christ sacrificed in this sacrament?' Aquinas asked, and replied,
1. No, it would seem. For it is written in *Hebrews* that *Christ by a single offering has perfected for all time those who are sanctified*. That offering was his sacrifice. Therefore he is not sacrificed in the celebration of this sacrament.
2. Moreover, Christ's sacrifice was made upon the cross;

107

He gave himself up for us, a fragrant offering and sacrifice to God. Now in the Mass Christ is not crucified. Neither, then, is he sacrificed.

3. Again, in Christ's sacrifice *priest and victim are the same*, as Augustine points out. Yet in the mass the priest and the victim are not the same. Therefore the celebration of this sacrament is not a sacrifice of Christ.''[5]

Nor was the eucharistic grace automatic, independent of the attitude of heart of the worshipper; – another Catholic myth that David had always believed.

"*Could the body of Christ as it is under this sacrament ever be seen by the eye?*" asked Aquinas finally.

"As long . . . as man is still on the way to heaven, he can only know it by faith, in the same way as other supernatural realities are known.''[3]

David's heartfelt 'Amen', almost broke the library silence. Whatever was all the fuss about? Here was sound Protestant teaching. If the vast majority of Catholics had believed something else, the Angelic Doctor could hardly be blamed. Other books taught David that many modern Catholics were coming to terms with this, and recognising that the classic doctrine of transubstantiation was a thirteenth-century way of describing the *spiritual* presence of Christ in the eucharist, something which all Protestants accept in varying degrees.[4] Catholics, then, were not so wide of the mark after all.

Twice during this period David visited the shrine of Our Lady of Walsingham in Norfolk. He was profoundly disturbed by much he saw at this centre of Marian devotion for Catholics in the Church of England. Then he met an Anglo-Catholic priest in Derby who had attended a renewal conference there. During the conference, while praying in the church which symbolised for David all that was mediaeval and reactionary in modern Catholicism, he had been gloriously baptised in the Spirit and had received the gift of tongues. His whole ministry had been transformed.

His bitter antagonism towards Protestants had disappeared. His hard and unbending way of life had softened and mellowed. If God could do that to a man in the shrine of Our Lady of Walsingham, perhaps God was not so bothered about external physical forms, after all.

Sometime later a Roman Catholic Renewal Weekend was held near Don's new home in Essex. They streamed in by hired coach from all over the area. Don went nervously to watch.

The large school hall, borrowed for the occasion, was festooned with bright banners, not mediaeval imitations with anaemic saints and virgins, but cheerful modern creations, featuring descending doves and flames and stylised figures with upraised hands. 'Christ is King', Don read. 'Jesus is Alive Today.' 'Come and Praise the Lord our King.' 'We are One in the Spirit.'

The bookstall carried titles by C. S. Lewis, Michael Green, John Stott, besides Catholic publications majoring on prayer, healing, group Bible-study and the work of the Holy Spirit. People hailed each other, hugged each other, sat clutching Bibles and smoking cigarettes. Several greeted Don with delight, reminding him how they had quite often dropped in on one of his Bible studies or Sunday evening evangelistic sermons. Often, he had never suspected they were Catholics at all. Above the hubbub, loudspeakers brought recorded music; dated CSSM choruses and Sankey hymns, more modern Scripture in song so characteristic of charismatic renewal. When about five hundred had crowded in, a small group with guitars and flutes took its place around a piano, a burly young priest who looked like a rugby player blew on to a microphone to attract attention, and the proceedings began.

"Welcome everyone, and praise the Lord!" the priest cried in the best 1950s 'Youth for Christ' manner. "We've got friends here from all over the county. Welcome to you all! But, best of all, we have the Lord Jesus Christ with us today. He promised, where two or three gathered in his name, he is in the midst. Isn't that wonderful? Let's welcome him!" And five hundred people gave a round of applause, interspersed with murmurs of "Praise God," and "Dear Jesus."

"Now, there's no need for a priest to run this today," he continued. "The Holy Spirit is here. He is the master of our worship. So I'll sit down, and you just worship as the spirit leads."

Suddenly it had turned from a Youth for Christ rally to a Brethren worship-meeting. Don knew enough about these, for they were the foundation of his Christian life and the background music to his childhood and teens: the hush of silent prayer, the rustle of pages as Bibles were opened, the quiet suggestion from someone that a hymn be sung or a chorus chanted, the slightly hesitant start to the music as people caught up with the song, constant reference to loved Scriptures read with brief comments by one person and another, the great doctrines of grace still raising wonder, love and praise, the hushed sense that Christ was here, he loved us and we loved him.

He brought me to the banqueting house,
   and his banner over me was love (Song of Solomon 2:4).

Don shook himself. Surely the resemblance was superficial. Surely, here were people sitting in rows without someone at the front, just asking for favourite hymns, a likeness of structure, or lack of it, and no more. That would not do, for it was not true. Not only the resemblance – the content also was the same.

> And can it be that I should gain
> An interest in the Saviour's blood?

one wanted to sing – Wesley's great conversion-hymn.

> Amazing grace, how sweet the sound
> That saved a wretch like me . . .

they sang, and several wept.

> I once was lost, but now I'm found,
> Was blind, but now I see.

A new hymn began each verse with a soft refrain of Alleluias . . .

> Spread the good news through all the world.
> Jesus has died and is risen.

To another chorus Don listened incredulously:

> I have been born again
> Through faith in Jesus Christ.

Then those Bibles, loved and treasured! Quite obviously the people were not used to reading them. That was a recent habit and a happy discovery. Often, when someone shared a few verses, many were seemingly hearing them for the first time. One read Romans, chapter 8. The great argument – no condemnation, walking in the Spirit, the Spirit bearing witness that we are children of God, election, predestination, calling, justification, glorification, the joyous crescendo, 'nothing can separate us' – was read with deep feeling and received with enthusiasm.

"This is the Word of the Lord," the reader concluded.

"Thanks be to God," they almost roared in response.

So the Scriptures tumbled out; Revelation 5, Ephesians 1, disconnected verses full of praise, joyful psalms, gospel assurances, visions of Christ. Sometimes it changed from a Brethren assembly to a Pentecostal praise-in. Several prophesied. One prayed in tongues while another interpreted. Many clapped their hands to the songs. In the enthusiasm of a new hymn, "Walk, walk in the Light", several rows of priests, nuns and layfolk stood, held hands and danced a kind of swaying shuffle.

> The Spirit comes to set men free,
>   Walk, walk in the Light.
> He binds us all in unity.
>   Walk, walk in the Light.

Then came that haunting ululation from one voice, caught up in harmony by others, until all joined in the soaring exaltation of singing in the Spirit.

Long before the end, Don was in tears, weeping quietly and steadily. Somehow, it seemed again like his conversion to Christ, twenty-five years before. Then, a brief adolescent rebellion against his parents' faith had led him into a wilderness, with no identity and no direction. No more dull attendance at breaking-of-bread and gospel meeting, for he refused to go. But what in its place? The self-conscious, immature atheism of his friends at school? Nothing better than that? He had stood on Redcar promenade during the final year of Hitler's war, and stared into the frosty night sky. Stars innumerable glowed and flickered in the black void above – Cassiopea, Pleiades, Orion. What did the books say? Some of those stars were so far away that, travelling at the speed of light, their image was reaching his eyes after five hundred years of travel. Some of them might not exist any longer, destroyed centuries before, their impact on his retina only an illusion. He could see things which did not exist.

Don had shivered. Whether they existed or not, they were so distant that it did not matter one way or the other. Cold, remote, inhuman, a universe largely made up of empty, freezing, soulless space: how could one person matter in such a cosmos? The earth was a speck. He was a speck on that speck. His hopes and fears, his ambitions and dreams, his very existence, signified nothing. He had shivered again and hurried home.

The warmth of the kitchen had greeted him. His father casually invited him to hear an evangelist at the Gospel Hall in a few days' time. Why not? He had not been for months. The decision that changed Don's life was sandwiched between some amateur philosophising about the size of the universe and the next radio instalment of a Paul Temple thriller.

The evangelist had arrived with a blizzard that blanketed the area in snow and brought transport to a standstill. Day after day, the flakes whirled and fell. A handful of people struggled to hear the small-time Elmer Gantry. Don heard nothing new. But somehow this was for him as it had never been before. The never-ending snow still fell as he plodded home. "Wash me, and I shall be whiter than snow" (Psalm 51:7)

> Come now, let us reason together,
>   says the LORD:
> though your sins are like scarlet,
>   they shall be as white as snow (Isaiah 1:18).
> Wash me in the blood of the Lamb, [they had sung,]
> And I shall be whiter than snow.

Don's thoughts whirled and danced as wildly as the snow in the wind. What should he do? This was more than the tug-of-war between the infant security of religion deeply rooted in his parent-images and the insecurity of his own free world. Indeed, security was his last thought. Towering over his consciousness was the figure of Jesus Christ the Lord, commanding, asking, pleading, demanding mastery of his life. He stood with a grace which did not wait until Don was what he should be, but came to him as he was. Then, almost imperceptibly, the struggle ended. No decision was necessary. No alternatives were left.

Twenty-five years of grammar school, industry, itinerant evangelism and the Baptist ministry had followed. A new-found facility with words and a warmth of communication had persuaded hundreds to accept life from the hands of Jesus, all within the circle where such things were normal, accepted and required; – Brethren assemblies, gospel missions and Baptist churches of the more evangelical type.

But now! Don woke with a start to find his face wet with tears. Now, he was sitting in a school hall surrounded by

Catholics – Catholics! – Roman Catholics! – who talked and felt, believed and sang in the same way as himself, unless his senses were totally deceiving.

Something had happened deep within him when Don drove home from the day of renewal. An almost physical weight had been lifted. It seemed as if he had been carrying round with him for years the personal burden of four-and-a-half centuries of Protestant-Catholic hatred and strife. Now it had gone. He found few who understood when he tried to explain. No doubt he expressed himself badly. One listener, much involved in charismatic renewal, listened thoughtfully and made a suggestion.

"I imagine that what has happened is something like this. The Spirit of God has said to you at some deep level, 'Nevertheless, their Father is yours.' "

Notes

¹Thomas Aquinas, *Summa Theologiae* (Eyre & Spottiswoode, 1964), Vol. 58, 55
²*ibid.*, Vol.59, 133
³*ibid.*, Vol.58, 117.
⁴For a fuller description of what Aquinas meant by transubstantiation see our *The Meal That Unites*? (Hodder & Stoughton, 1981), 75-8.

CHAPTER 16 – ONE IN THE SPIRIT

"'Their Father is yours.' That's it! That's it exactly!" mused Don. He sat pondering his friend's assessment of the Catholic renewal rally. Their dogma, in parts, might be up the pole, their hierarchy, to a Brethren-cum-Baptist, repulsive, the claims of their priests unfounded, and their cruelties in history enormous. All that mattered no longer. The way those Catholics had worshipped God, rejoiced in his word and shared their joy with each other left Don with no alternative; he and they alike were all children of one Father.

Don felt rather like the apostle Peter after his visit to Cornelius in Acts chapter ten. He, too, had gone to people with whom he had shared a lifetime of suspicion. The Romans, like Catholics against Protestants, had committed unspeakable atrocities against the Jews. By entering Cornelius's home and sharing his food, Peter had risked losing his closest friends. Yet the Spirit had been outpoured. Cornelius, his family and his friends had praised God in tongues. "If then God gave the same gift to them as he gave to us," Peter argued, "when we believed in the Lord Jesus Christ, who was I that I could withstand God?" When the Jerusalem Christians heard this they were silenced. And they glorified God, saying, "Then to the Gentiles also God has granted repentance unto life" (Acts 11:17,18).

The earliest Christians were in no doubt. A Christian was someone who, in baptism, had publicly confessed Jesus as Lord. In his heart he believed that God had raised Jesus from the dead. In his life he displayed the power of the Holy Spirit and was glad to belong to the local company of believers, the church. For three hundred years there were few problems with that simple combination of faith and action. Constant persecution made certain that few became

115

Christians for the wrong reasons. The apostles' letters held widely scattered groups together in allegiance to one body, one spirit, one hope, one Lord, one faith, one baptism, one God and father of all, who is above all, through all and in all (see Ephesians 4:4-6). Any who strayed from the truth of the gospel could easily be recalled to the apostles' teaching, handed down from Jesus himself.

In time, however, all kinds of weirdos claimed to be following the apostles' teaching. Some were half-Christian. Some were not Christians at all, even though they talked a lot about Jesus. How were people to know the difference between true Christians and false? The answer increasingly given was that true Christians accepted the rule of a bishop who could trace his descent, through an unbroken line of bishops, to one of the apostles of Jesus himself. All true Christians accepted this idea of 'apostolic succession'. The foundations of the 'catholic' church were laid, the world-wide community of Christian believers linked to Jesus and his disciples through their bishops.

At last, in the year 312, the on-off persecutions of the previous two hundred and fifty years finally came to an end. Constantine became Roman Emperor. The Edict of Milan granted Christians freedom of worship. State grants enabled impressive church buildings to be erected. By the end of the fourth century Christianity became the official religion of the Empire. Thousands flocked into the church, while those who remained outside were persecuted in turn.

But true Christianity, as we have shown, is a delicate union of inward faith and outward action. Belief in the resurrection is displayed in baptism. New life in Jesus is expressed in membership of the church. At any time it is possible to have one without the other. The first Samaritan Christians were baptised before they received the Holy Spirit (see Acts 8). Cornelius, on the other hand, was filled with the Holy Spirit and then baptised (see Acts 10:44-48). And in the fourth-century rush to join the church, the emphasis was inevitably placed on the outward actions rather than on the inward faith. Sadly, even Christian leaders were carried away with excitement. Many declared that baptism and regular attendance at Holy Communion were all that was necessary, indeed, essential, to make someone a true Christian. Of course, there were always many who enjoyed the inward change of the Holy Spirit, as well. Revivial movements flourished both inside and outside the ranks of the official Catholic Church. But from the year one thousand onwards the general idea was that a Christian was someone who was born in a particular part of the world, and who was baptised, and who went to Communion. The demands of personal faith and the inner work of the Holy Spirit were largely forgotten over large areas of Christendom.

At first, the Reformation in the sixteenth century promised to set things right. For a start the reformers rejected the idea of apostolic succession. Bishops could not guarantee true Christianity, for even bishops could lose the truth of the gospel. True apostolic succession, the reformers said, was found not in lines of bishops, but in obedience to the teaching of God's word. Therefore, the reformers demanded faith as well as baptism in all true Christians. But they only succeeded where they had the support of the local king or prince. For most people, this simply meant that they exchanged one kind of religion (Catholic) for another (one type of Protestantism). Christians were still people who were born in particular places and who were baptised. Only the anabaptists consistently demanded personal faith in a living Saviour who transforms the believer by the power of his Spirit. For their brave stand, they were persecuted and punished, and largely destroyed.

In England, the Evangelical awakening in the eighteenth century, renewed the demand in all true Christians for personal faith and an experience of salvation. In themselves, the Evangelicals insisted, baptism, confirmation and regular attendance at Holy Communion did not and could not make people Christians. Only the power of the Holy Spirit, received by faith, could do that.

Not surprisingly, the evangelical message was not always well received. Formal religion always has some popular appeal, and its followers find the extra demands of 'heart religion' offensive. Evangelicals were pilloried and parodied. Many left the Church of England for the new Methodist churches and revitalised Free Churches. Even there, as those churches became increasingly respectable, Evangelicals tended to become isolated minorities.

Nevertheless, evangelical Christianity has remained a powerful force in Great Britain, the countries of her former Empire, the Americas, and the third world. The worldwide decline of formal religion in the twentieth century and renewed persecution of Christians in many parts of the world have given Evangelicals growing influence in many different Christian churches. On the whole, only those with personal faith in a living Saviour have been able on the one hand to resist the advance of secularism, and on the other to endure the rigours of persecution. Pentecostal and charismatic Christianity is a natural development of evangelical Christianity, even though some Evangelicals have bitterly opposed it.

Charismatic renewal in the Roman Catholic Church is therefore highly significant. To be sure, there has always been room for personal faith in that church, though Roman Catholics themselves would probably admit that it has rarely been expected or required outside the specific religious vocations of the priesthood and the communities. Now it is a growing movement among priests, monks and nuns and increasing numbers of lay folk.

What reduced Don to tears at the day of renewal was the realisation that the Roman Catholic folk with whom he was sitting and who were worshipping God so enthusiastically had been born again and filled with the Spirit as he himself had been. For them, the baptism of the Spirit was evangelical conversion. They might not call it that, but that, in effect, was what they had received.

Roman Catholic charismatic renewal therefore poses massive questions for Catholics and Protestants alike. "What makes an authentic Christian?" asks the Belgian Cardinal Leon Suenens. "A personal, saving encounter with Jesus, the Lord, the one who baptises in the Holy Spirit,"[1] he replies. "Conversion, baptism, encounter with

Jesus as Lord and Saviour, receiving the Holy Spirit, are all parts of a unique whole, a complex reality. Tradition calls it 'Christian initiation', 'enlightenment', 'entrance into a new life.' "[2]

Now if an authentic Christian is someone who has had a personal, saving encounter with Jesus, and if people inside and outside the Roman Catholic Church are enjoying such encounters, what effect does that have on traditional Catholic insistence that all true Christians must be baptised into that church? To be sure, the Second Vatican Council recognised other Christians as 'separated brethren', but can brethren, conscious of a common sonship in Christ, be separated?

Future, visible unity, Cardinal Suenens insists, must find its focus in the Spirit, for "It is the Spirit who unites us in the acclamation 'Jesus is Lord.'"[3] The Spirit inspired the Scriptures and continues to illumine the church to understand them.[4] The Spirit is the 'we' of the Father and the Son, and the 'we' of the body of Christ. Thus "the Holy Spirit is, at the heart of the Church, creating a unity that transcends our calculations."[5] Within that unity there will be great diversity, but Christ will build his church and the gates of Hades shall not prevail against it (Matthew 16:18, and note).

What, then, of the exclusive claims of the Catholic priesthood to be the only validly ordained Christian ministry? What of the claims of the Bishop of Rome to speak *ex cathedra*, and to define and redefine Christian belief in infallibility? What of the widespread fragmentation within Protestantism, and the exclusive attitude of many groups towards those with whom they disagree on secondary, let alone primary, issues? And what of Mary, revered by Catholics – some would say to the point of worship equal and even superior to Christ himself, yet neglected among Protestants?

The Cardinal is encouraged by moves towards government by council in the Roman Church, hoping they will remove something of the stumbling-block (to Protestants) of the position of an infallible pope. He makes constructive suggestions about the place of Mary in Christian devotion, insisting that her role as the mother of our Lord gives her an inevitable position in the scheme of redemption. That place, however, is always under the sovereignty of the Holy Spirit. He filled her with himself before Jesus was born, and inspired her to 'magnify the Lord'. Thus, Mary became the first charismatic![6]

Visible unity will not be realised tomorrow, nor the day after. The Belgian is only one in a whole college of cardinals. Despite their impressive strength in parts of North America, charismatics are only a tiny minority among Roman Catholics all over the world, as they are in most other churches. Currently, in the Roman Church, there is something of a reaction to the heady liberalism of post-Vatican II. Among charismatics, too, the enthusiasm of the early pioneers has ebbed to a degree. The one movement may be splintering into several – Catholic renewal, Anglican renewal, Methodist renewal and so on. Some charismatics have already separated from the parent churches which gave them birth. That is particularly sad, for today's new discoveries always become tomorrow's arid traditions. There are enough disparate denominations already without more being added to the list.

Nevertheless, things will never be the same again. Throughout the church all over the world, authentic Christianity is being defined, less in terms of membership of a visible organisation, and more in terms of personal commitment to a reigning, sovereign Lord. Christians of every kind are exploring their common faith rather than insisting on their differences. Bitterness and prejudice may remain in Northern Ireland, but there the conflict is more racial than religious. And even there, Catholics and Protestants are finding reconciliation and peace, unity, love and joy under the sovereign renewing work of the Holy Spirit.

"There is one body and one Spirit . . . one hope that belongs to your call, one Lord, one faith, one baptism, one God and Father of us all, who is above all and through all and in all" (Ephesians 4:4,5). Through charismatic renewal, God has shown the twentieth-century church the way to the realisation of that unity. Despite the questions which remain, he has reconciled Christians who were previously most deeply divided. Will the church in the twenty-first century follow where renewed Christians have led? Or will it sink back into stagnation and decay?

Notes

[1]Leon Joseph Cardinal Suenens, *A New Pentecost?* (Darton, Longman & Todd, 1975), 121.
[2]*ibid.*
[3]*ibid.*,185.
[4]*ibid.*, 189.
[5]*ibid.*, 193.
[6]*ibid.*, 196-211.

CHAPTER 17 – MAKING DISCIPLES

"I'm leaving the ministry, Don," a colleague confided, sadly, one day. "I really don't see any point in staying any longer." Stubbornness and self-pity were written on his face. "Life is just a series of half-done tasks, when I know full well that someone else can do them better."

"Oh, come on . . ." Don protested.

He held up his hand. "Listen. A couple come to me with marriage problems. I listen. But the folk at the Marriage Guidance place have more experience. Someone brings me an emotional problem. I dabble in it, but the psychiatrist is far better qualified."

"What about the youth work?" Don smiled.

"Well, what about it? A hand-to-mouth affair if ever there was one! And down the road the Council have sunk thousands in a new Youth Centre with a paid leader."

"Oh, come on," Don rejoined again. "Didn't you notice that National Opinion Poll last week? Who is the most useful member of the public? Clergymen headed the list, followed closely by doctors and teachers, with politicians well in the rear."

The friend shook his head impatiently. "Secular man . . ."

"Secular man, my foot!" Don retorted aggressively. He had been looking at some of the experiments of South Bank religion, as the Press called it. Churches south of the Thames had been persuaded to close down and unite in an ecumenical scheme dominated by the theology of a bishop and a rector who seemed to believe that the ways in which a Cambridge academic and an East End docker thought were identical.

"There's no such animal trotting around with 'Secular Man' printed on his chest. Someone's been looking at too many atheistic professors. Look at your average man in South Shields. He thinks God exists, but he doesn't know him. He sometimes prays, but rarely sees an answer. He believes there is life after death but is hazy about the details. He expects Christians to be 'different', and sniggers at trendy parsons who drop in for a self-conscious beer. One of his main fears is that if he goes to church the roof will fall in.

"Now they are not the problems of a secular man, whoever he is supposed to be. They are the problems of a confused man, rather superstitious and with lots of reservations about slick answers from self-styled specialists. You will find working-class people untouched by organised religion, yet sensitive to the implications of marriage, birth, suffering and death. I am visiting them every day. You will find middle-class folk who now have most of the things they once wanted, yet who are puzzled to find they are still not satisfied. A sensitive and alert minister backed by a wide-awake church can bring a new dimension to these people's lives in a way no official of the Welfare State can ever do. Sorry, pal. I really am sorry. I'm starting to preach a sermon. I'll keep it for Sunday."

Don's friend left the ministry, as he had threatened, and moved into teaching. A few miles further north, another example of 'secular evangelism" (*sic*) was an even worse failure, and that minister moved on to the safe halls of a theological college. Both of them were succeeded by men of spiritual power, committed to dynamic, Bible-centred preaching. Both churches flourished again. On the South Bank the same thing happened. *Failure of a Mission* was the honest title of a subsequent report. The rector at the heart of the experiment won renown for his remark that the nearest they ever got to New Testament fellowship was in the church building they turned into a bingo-hall. From such councils of despair we in Sunderland steadfastly turned away.

Because we had learned that the church is a body, with every member, like the body's limbs and organs, fulfilling a different function, we quickly realised that evangelism was the task of the whole church, and not just of its minister and one or two specialists. Since ninety-five per cent of the British people no longer sit dutifully under the sound of the gospel at 6.30 p.m. each Sunday evening, Christians must take the gospel to the people first. And that task is far too great for the minister alone.

It is, of course, the New Testament pattern. In the Temple in Jerusalem, the market-place in Antioch, the synagogue in Corinth, the lecture-room at Ephesus, the 'open university' at Athens, and from house to house, the first Christians preached, not sermons, but explanations to already interested and puzzled listeners. They explained why a once-lame man was leaping around, why a crazy, fortune-telling girl had become sane and normal, why they had become involved in a riot, why sacred statues annoyed them, why they couldn't care less about racial differences, why their own lives had been turned inside out. Is there a quality in Christians' lives today which demands the same explanation, the assertion that Jesus Christ is alive?

As more and more of the Christians at Enon entered into the fullness of the Spirt and exercised different gifts, so that opportunities for witness and evangelism multiplied. One member joined the young wives in her area for a regular coffee morning. After weeks of normal small-talk, the conversation turned to religion. Because they were confused she offered to invite her minister along the following week to answer questions. As a result, Don spent two hours dealing with age-old problems: Why does God allow suffering? Is there purpose in life? What should I teach my children? How does prayer work? What happens when you die? Only one other member of that group attended church regularly.

A teachers' association was concerned about the drug problem amongst school children. Don was invited to speak for an hour on how to recognise the symptoms of abuse, and what a Christian message has to offer in the way of cure. How? Because one Christian teacher took his extra-curricular activities seriously.

Another member joined the Community Association of

a new housing estate. Through personal conversation and the sharing of problems at committee meetings, the treasurer and chairman both attended an Easter baptismal service. "I've never seen anything like it in my life," one of them said afterwards. "There's something there, and I want it." Both were subsequently baptised.

Sixty students, two-thirds of them non-Christian, gathered in a lecturer's house to hear a Jew and a Communist criticise the church for twenty minutes each. Don had another twenty minutes in which to reply, after which the floor was anyone's for another hour. This happened because the lecturer was a practising Christian, fully involved in college life.

Sixth-formers at David's school became equally fascinated by and scornful of the ouija-board and spiritualism. One night after school, thirty of them stayed to hear a prominent medium and Don debate the relevant issues.

Student members of the Christian Union at the local polytechnic adopted Don as their pastor and Enon as their spiritual home. Then, since no one else seemed to have any great interest in them, they arranged with a slightly surprised Principal to invent a position for Don which gave him access at any time to the residential quarters. "Come and have dinner at the top table once a week," he suggested. "Say grace – a thing I never like to do – and afterwards meet the students informally over coffee and answer their questions."

Feeling rather nervous, Don passed through a hushed student commonroom on his first visit. A slag-heap, built from waste from nearby coal-mines, had slid down a mountainside in South Wales, enfulfing a school and burying a hundred and twenty children alive. The early evening television news was bringing graphic pictures of the tragedy. There was no shortage of questions after dinner that night.

On subsequent visits, atheists, Hindus, Jews, agnostics and Christians waded into each other on communism, abortion, black magic, the faults of the church, the failure of the Welfare State, life after death and so on. Then on

125

occasional Sunday evenings it was easy to organise 'student sermons' in the church. Students were invited to tea by church members and brought along to the service. This particularly pleased Norwegians, East Africans and Indians. Deliberately provocative sermons were preached on 'The Student Revolution', 'Is Christianity Escapism?' 'Faith in God in a Scientific Age'. Afterwards, respectable members of the congregation were sent home (unless curiosity held them), while at a 'coffee and talkback' the students were given the right to reply. The device rarely failed to lead to at least one outright conversion. Numbers of others also became regular attenders.

Philip was typical. A nominal Methodist whose religion was a dash of socialism with a slight flavour of God, he objected to the 'emotional' character of the sermon. Later, he admitted it had spoken to him. After a face-to-face encounter with Jesus, he became a fervent evangelist, returning two years later to his home church with a new message and a new master.

Pat debated one religious, moral and ethical topic after another for three months before being challenged with her personal response to the character of Christ. Three weeks later she rang Don from a call-box, her voice trembling with emotion. "I'd like you to be the first to know. I've just come from a house-group. I know what I want. Jesus Christ is my Saviour." Her course ended, she found employment in the area, joined the church, and became one of its most effective youth leaders.

Now there is no suggestion that renewal taught us to evangelise for the first time. Don had been deeply and successfully committed to what our forefathers called 'soul-winning' long before he had any charismatic experience. At fair-ground and factory-gates, race-courses and resorts, city squares and village greens, he had stood with a colleague and spoken of a living Saviour to passing people. Techniques had been shaped, prayers offered, sermons preached, and things had happened. People had been confronted with Christ in the unlikeliest of places, and bowed the knee to him. David, too, was totally convinced

126

that no apologies were needed for an old-fashioned gospel, and was seeking to master the art of teaching the scriptures in school with relevance. All this had happened before any contact with renewal.

What the Sunderland experience did was to anchor evangelism in the local church. That meant much more than the church building providing a convenient pulpit and a docile audience. Don had moved on from a church in nearby Newcastle with an uneasy suspicion that he had made exactly that mistake. The gratifying growth in the congregation slowed as soon as he left.

The whole pattern in Sunderland indicated something very different. Grim days had passed in a borrowed building with a congregation of fifteen faithfuls. But faithful they were, and they looked and prayed for better days. A few key people moved into the area. A commitment to a more Bible-based faith developed. Members began to look for a man with vision to lead them. Circumstances changed, and a fine new building was erected. The preacher at the official opening spoke prophetically of "God's man for this church, not far away, prepared by him and waiting for you to find him." Renewal began as early as that, when the Bible took on new importance, past defeats were forgotten and mere survival-thinking was abandoned.

Don's new hopes of popular exposition, pastoral evangelism and contemporary worship found a ready response. They needed to, for none of them were possible without people to pastor, a congregation to worship, and a community to express its faith.

That was the new evangelism. It sprang from a body of people committed to each other in happy discovery and eventful worship, sharing a restlessness to make Christ known.

CHAPTER 18 – RENEWAL, TODAY
AND TOMORROW

Twenty years ago renewal burst afresh on the Christian Church. It was a movement composed of several different elements. In fact it was not a 'Movement' in any organised sense, but simply a *move* . . . a surge of conviction and experiment and change and action, which touched every continent.

Partly it was a protest. Church bureaucracy was seen to be helpless to combat arrogant atheism. Middle-class morality was powerless to stem the tide of permissiveness. A half-secular theology of social tinkering had nothing to say against the threat of resurgent paganism and occult powers. Even sound doctrine seemed empty of the heart-warming power once associated with its great credal confessions. Out of a reaction against such half-Christianities the hunger for renewal sprang.

The hunger led to a number of different emphases. One element was a return to biblical certainties and personal life-changing encounter with God. That has almost marked out the Evangelical. Another element was a seeking after eventful corporate worship, shared devotion, and new kinds of community life. That too is biblical, but more often thought of as Catholic. And there has been also a fresh exploring of the supernatural, the phenomenal, the inspirational, the charismatic and the prophetic. That trend we think of as Pentecostal. But is has as much biblical support and as many historical precedents as the Evangelical and the Catholic.

Anyone who wants to understand the church that has entered the 1980s must know something of this stirring. For it is shared by every brand of Christianity in every continent. From America to Australia, from Scotland to South Africa, in churches Catholic, Protestant and third-world, it can be seen and heard and felt. All share a surge of new life which expresses itself in elements as diverse as evangelical conversion, radical discipleship, speaking in tongues, community life, biblical preaching, liturgical reform, social protest, and millenial hope.

It can be thoroughly disturbing to Christians who like everything in neat packages. The wrapping keeps getting undone and the contents keep getting mixed up.

But there is really nothing new about any of this. We only think there is because we read both Bible accounts and church history (if we read the second at all) through a haze of our own upbringing or limited convictions which both colours and distorts.

Many Catholics, for example, are vaguely aware of reform and renewal movements in their own history, but allocate them comfortably to the past or wrap them respectably in monks' habits and miss the challenge. Protestants know of past 'revival' movements which they rightly associate with a 'return to the Bible' but wrongly assume to have been uniform and safely reformed. The great Puritan revivals certainly fit that pattern, but neither the Moravian Pentecost of Europe nor the Wesleyan revival of Britain and America were so obliging.

The passage of time makes for comfort. Catholics forget (or do not know) that the papacy almost rejected Francis of Assisi when it rejected Peter of Waldo. Protestants find it difficult to understand or believe that the Puritans' successors would have nothing to do with John Wesley, that John Knox's successors condemned D. L. Moody, that Lutherans were shocked and scandalised by the Moravians, and that Calvinistic and Modernistic Baptists combined in rejecting (for opposite reasons) the Baptist revivalist Charles Spurgeon.

What we all fail to notice when it happens again is that it has happened before. The history of Christendom is shot through with recurrent periods of new life and advance and self-challenge, variously called reformation, revival or renewal. The *ingredients* are always recognisably the same. The *proportional mixture* of the ingredients differs greatly.

Montanism in the second century protested against formalism, and renewed the prophetic element. Monastic and revival movements in the Middle Ages protested against worldliness and majored on radical life-style. The sixteenth century Reformation focused on the return to scripture, and the freeness of the grace of God. The eighteenth-century awakening majored on heart-experience (John Wesley's 'heart strangely warmed'). Twentieth-century Catholic Renewal is recalling its people to personal faith, prayer and Bible-study. Pentecostalism emphasises spiritual power and charismatic gift. But all alike are catching some of the broken beams and refracted rays of that total work of him who is light of the world. Or, as one perceptive and scholarly observer has written, "the Christian life is being offered in diverse packages, but what is inside is the same – newness of life in Christ."

Has the present movement passed its peak, as many believe? It would be more accurate to say that its first phase is well past. The astonishment of rediscovery and reawakening is over, and the hard work of translating it into deeds for the 1980s is well under way. Unavoidably, the first freshness of those early days, when everything was so new and unexpected, had faded a little. There is no purpose in trying to re-create the exact feeling. As C. S. Lewis once said of conversion, a high tide is sometimes needed to get a ship into dry dock, but once it is inside, the repairs and restructuring are more important than the excitement of getting in. That repairing and restructuring is now well under way.

This book makes a modest contribution to the record of those first exciting days. The authors look back to them, not to repeat them but to record gratitude to God for what He began. Their own experience has gone forward since then, and they understand more now than they did then about the implications. They are still exploring, and things are still happening – more now than then! This final chapter reflects on some of those implications.

Renewal's place in the life of the church today is beyond question. Within the United Kingdom alone, almost the

130

only churches to have seen significant growth during the past twenty years are those which have learned from the charismatic movement. Any movement which can reverse the numerical decline of the last half-century demands serious attention. Beyond specific charismatic churches, renewal has touched the church as a whole with permanent effects.

Renewal has taught Christian people, clerical and lay, the importance of a personal relationship with God. "Holy Spirit, I want whatever you've got going for me!" prayed Richard Hare when, as Bishop of Pontefract, he knelt at the altar-rail in a Festival of Praise. There, as he knelt, he was overwhelmed with a sense of God's love and God's presence as never before. In the months and years that followed, the Bible came alive, prayer was enjoyed and power was supplied for his episcopal service.

The bishop's story is completely typical of that of hundreds who have been touched by charismatic renewal. Indeed, in its early days, this was just about all the movement attempted. However the baptism of the Spirit may be theologically defined, in practice it results in a new sense of the reality of God and of the Christian's adopted sonship in Christ. Dejected with the dull routine of defeated Christian lives, tired out with fruitless Christian service, frustrated by the monotonous aridity of so-called Christian worship, thousands found new life and fresh hope in the baptism of the Spirit. Although today the horizons are wider, Spirit-baptism remains the basis of charismatic activity and commitment.

Because evangelical Christians had always demanded the sense of a personal relationship with God as the basis for Christian commitment and service, they found charismatic renewal totally confusing. What could it possibly offer that they did not possess already? Doubts about Pentecostal theology had caused most of them to reject the baby with the bath-water. A century of survival warfare against the heady forces of theological Modernism had left them with a sense of stubborn pride; nobody outside their pedigree could possibly teach them anything. Non-biblical

131

strata in their tradition concerning gifts had clouded their otherwise accurate biblical understanding; gifts were never intended to survive the apostolic period. So how could renewal be the work of the Spirit of God? With all those forces we struggled in *Spiritual Gifts and the Church*. Not charismatic enough for some, too charismatic for others, we helped hundreds all over the world, who had reservations like our own to a new understanding of God's renewal of the church. The saddest Christians we know today are devout evangelicals who are trying to carry on as if charismatic renewal had never happened; by and large the Spirit's tide has flowed round them and passed them by.

Renewal has not only taught the importance of a personal relationship with God. It has also sparked off a new interest in the theology of the Holy Spirit. Twenty years ago the Holy Spirit was the forgotten person of the Trinity. As James Dunn observed, in the Catholic tradition he had been subordinated to the church; in the Protestant tradition he had been subordinated to the Bible.[1] All that has now changed. Christians all over the world are keen not only to experience the Spirit, but also to explore every facet of his nature and to make him known to others.

Renewal has also restored the supernatural dimension to Christian activity. "The day of miracles is not past," declares the charismatic Christian. "Jesus Christ is the same yesterday and today and for ever" (Hebrews 13:8). "He who believes in me will also do the works that I do; and greater works than these will he do, because I go to the Father" (John 14:12). So the annals of the movement are filled with stories of people who have been dramatically healed from terminal medical conditions, from psychosomatic illnesses and psychological disorders. Others claim to have been delivered from demon possession, while still others have claimed insight into situations of which they had no natural knowledge.

Herein, perhaps, lies the secret of much of the attractiveness of charismatic renewal, and herein also perhaps, lies its greatest danger. The New Testament itself witnesses to the dramatic effect of supernatural activity, but also describes how people were drawn to Christ for the wrong reasons (John 6:26). It warns of the dangers of exalting supernatural gifts above the supernatural grace of love (1 Corinthians 13:1,2). It prophesies doom on those who exercise supernatural powers without first giving obedience to Christ (Matthew 7:21-23). And what happens when expected miracles fail to occur and earnest prayer for divine intervention apparently goes unanswered?

Nevertheless, Christians worship a God who became incarnate in Christ, a God who raised Jesus from the dead and a God who through the Holy Spirit in the early church "turned the world upside down" (Acts 17:6). People flock to charismatic gatherings and charismatic churches because they are expecting something to happen. That, surely, is better than going out of habit, or not going at all because everything is so predictable and boring.

More importantly than anything else, however, renewal has restored to the church the concept of the body of Christ. The Christian church is not an association of individuals who meet together from time to time, in order to worship Jesus individually. Nor is it a secular club devoted to the propagation of religion. It is a living organism with Christ as its head, and its members are the different limbs and organs. All should work together harmoniously for the good of all.

This corporate understanding of the church has been a healthy corrective to the undue individualism which has marked Christian life and activity for the past two hundred years. Its effects have been widespread throughout the life of the church.

First, it has enabled Christians to share together in the church's worship. In the best charismatic circles worship is no longer something conducted by the minister, to which the people listen, merely joining in as directed. "When you come together, each one has a hymn, a lesson, a revelation, a tongue, or an interpretation . . . so that all may learn and all be encouraged" (1 Corinthians 14:26,31). Thus many can take part, each bringing his own particular contribution as the Spirit leads. This has often resulted in quite new ingredients, until recently not normally associated with Christian worship. Charismatic churches have often led the way in introducing dance and drama into worship. When these are sensitively and ably presented they add a new dimension to Christian worship whereby the worshippers' hearts are lifted into the presence of God. New songs of worship have made praise a reality in many congregations where before it was a formality. Simple songs of adoration and commitment, directly addressed to the Father, to Jesus and to the Holy Spirit, have begun to free the church from the strait-jacket of eighteenth- and nineteenth-century music and verse, and have given to worship a contemporary immediacy which is most refreshing. For all this to be realised, positive contributions are required from far more people than previously. As many become responsible for the depth and quality of Christian worship, so their self-esteem is enhanced and encouraged. Leaders, of course, are still there. They maintain decency and order. They are alive and sensitive to the Spirit, and they gently guide the worship from one phase to the next. But the old-fashioned monologue has gone, or should have done.

Secondly, understanding the church as the body of Christ has enabled Christians to share together in its leadership. Throughout most mainline denominations of the Western church, spiritual leadership has become largely confined in each congregation to one, or a few, specially ordained 'professionals'. They have been required to do everything: preach, preside at the eucharist, visit, teach, evangelise and so on. Consequently, the life or otherwise of different congregations has been directly related to the personal qualities of the minister or priest. Because no individual possesses all God's gifts, every ministry is deficient to some extent in one area or another.

In many charismatic churches all this is now changing. The full-time professionals are still present, but many are commissioning elders to share in spiritual oversight, besides more traditional assistance with administrative tasks. Achieving this new style of spiritual leadership has not always been easy. Serious teething troubles have often been encountered. But where it has worked it has enabled different elders to exercise different gifts, and a more whole and balanced ministry has resulted. When the professional has left, the church's ministry has continued and developed until a successor has arrived, instead of being barely maintained in limbo as before.

Thirdly, recognising that the church is the body of Christ has profoundly affected the quality of its fellowship. Christians are not intended to be snooker or pool balls which click against each other once a week on Sundays, but brothers and sisters in Christ, relating and sharing together in the deepest areas of their lives. Renewed Christians have discovered a new desire to help each other in trouble, to pray and learn together in their homes as well as in the sanctuary of church buildings. In many churches touched by renewal, members have taken seriously, the biblical concept of tithing, with dramatic effects on the churches' financial condition.

In some churches the sharing has gone further still, with whole families pledging themselves to each other to share their material resources and to exercise their gifts together for the benefit of the church and the wider community. Some have welcomed other Christians into their families at minimal cost, thus releasing them for full-time service for a limited or longer period. We have written little of this development of Christian households and communities for, as yet, it has not been part of our direct experience, but we rejoice at news of it happening elsewhere and pointing to an alternative Christian life-style for the future.

Fourthly, churches which function as the body of Christ find their outreach to the world enhanced. Evangelism is a specific gift enjoyed by relatively few, but all Christians can witness in different ways to the reality of the risen Christ. Churches which have learned to be living communities of Spirit-filled Christians have become attractive to the lost, not merely by the power of their preaching, but also by the quality of their love and genuine concern. Evangelism is no longer merely a preaching activity, but Christians loving each other and their neighbours with a winsome and genuine quality which can reach the hardest of hearts. This is the spiritual revival for which we pray, revival which stems from renewed Christians in renewed churches being the body of Christ in the world.

Fifthly, if individual congregations are the body of Christ, so is the whole church. Charismatic renewal has provided an impetus to the ecumenical movement from the grass-roots. At a time when many carefully-laid schemes for unity devised by church leaders have foundered, renewal has given Christians a unity in Christ which overcomes their traditional hostilities and suspicions. Problems indeed remain. Many on both sides of the Catholic/Protestant divide are grieved at their continuing inability to share the eucharist. But renewal has shown that unity is spiritual and not organisational. Unity is not uniformity. Although visible unity is desirable, the Spirit of God has never been confined to one or more particularly acceptable structures.

Of course, charismatic renewal has had its casualties. Spiritual revival always does. "Your adversary the devil prowls around like a roaring lion, seeking someone to devour" (1 Peter 5:8). Counterfeit gifts, enthusiasm to excess, exaggerated claims have characterised renewal in every era of the church's life.

Some Christians have seen charismatic Christianity as offering a short cut to effective ministry. They have imagined that the gifts of prophecy and tongues have absolved them from the need to prepare their sermons, Bible studies or any other programmes of Christian teaching and service. Such talk is more than dangerous. It not only presumes on the goodness of God! it is also a short step from laziness. A disciplined approach to preparation and a willingness to let the Spirit speak and guide as he wills are both required. Prayer and study will always be necessary. Only so will the Spirit be free.

To others, renewal has seemed to offer a short cut to spiritual authority. Particularly sad have been those situations in which charismatic Christians have denounced existing leadership as 'unspiritual', and have themselves attempted to take over. Others have tried, through sup-

136

posed prophecy, to give detailed guidance on marriage, employment and so on. But there is no short cut to authority in the church. Leaders in the early church were only appointed after fasting and prayer. Equally, today, self-appointed leaders are usually disastrous. True leaders mostly shrink from their new responsibilities.

Renewal has also seemed to promise to some a short cut to true spirituality. Praying in tongues has sometimes been regarded as the primary mark of divine approval. But love is what matters, and without it gifts are discordant and useless. A disciplined devotional life will always be necessary to true spirituality. The baptism of the Spirit should produce such discipline, and not excuse it.

Charismatic renewal burst on the church twenty years ago with all the exciting promise of a spring dawn. Spontaneously and independently throughout the world, Christians in different places and from widely divergent traditions became deeply conscious of their sonship in Christ. Praying in tongues and gifts of healing were rediscovered. The Bible came alive, worship was revitalised, and prayer became a joy instead of a duty. Most excitingly of all, Christians came together to worship, to pray and to express their new-found unity in the Spirit. One of David's most thrilling experiences at this time came when he attended a conference in Newcastle as an Anglican, enjoyed searching biblical exposition of the highest quality from a Baptist, and sat enthralled at the realisation that Roman Catholics were learning with him with direct eagerness, as well. Equally thrilling and reassuring was the insistence of many of the early charismatic leaders that, with their new discoveries, they would remain within their existing churches, praying that through their presence and influence God would touch the whole of their traditions as he had touched themselves.

Today, charismatic renewal stands at the crossroads. In some places where the fires of renewal once burned strongly the flame has been reduced to glowing embers. Elsewhere, the movement that promised to bring Christians together in vital unity in the Spirit is dividing back into its denominational strata. More denominational renewal events are now being held and fewer ecumenical ones. Yet unity in the Spirit is the only true basis for Christian unity. If charismatic Christians cannot give practical demonstration of that unity, what hope is there for the rest of the church?

Nor has the movement always remained within the traditional denominational boundaries. Already, several new charismatic groups are assuming denominational status, however stoutly they may deny it. Linked by magazines and other formal ties of membership, they are sometimes adopting an exclusive stance, to all intents and purposes excommunicating those with whom they do not agree.

This is a development we cannot support. The history of the Christian church is littered with breakaway groups demanding freedom from the restraints of their older traditions. They flourish for a while until their new insights in their turn become fossilised traditions, and their once-found freedom becomes as rigid as the tradition they have left.

Today, this kind of thing is happening once more in some of the emerging branches of the House-Church Movement. Rigid patterns of discipline, for example, threaten Christians with detailed control of their lives by appointed 'shepherds' far in excess of the proper authority of leaders which the New Testament allows. Freed also from the restraints necessarily imposed by denominational structures, some of the house churches are falling easy prey to charismatic extremism. Stories of exorcisms that have failed, healings that do not bear close examination, mental and physical breakdowns induced through pressure to speak in tongues often emanate from some of these churches. They bring dishonour to the name of Christ and the sovereign activity of the Holy Spirit. They give ready excuse for people to dismiss all charismatic renewal as emotionalism and extremism, to deny all charismatic gifts as being counterfeit.

Yet charismatic abuse and excess never justify rejecting the benefits of renewal. Where gifts and insights are abused they should be corrected, not rejected. That has been the mistake so often in the past. We live in times of radical

138

change. Patterns of political power, social structures, educational methods are all changing rapidly. Technological advance threatens traditional employment-patterns across whole nations and continents. Racial ferment stirs the world. Over all looms the long, dark shadow of nuclear and chemical warfare, threatening the very future of the human race itself. At such a time renewal poses fundamental questions.

What is the church? A religious club? A voluntary get-together of converts? Or something awesome, eternal and beautiful which God is shaping as a spectacle to men, demons and angels?

What is the Bible? An interesting record of man's religious quest in the Judaic and early Christian traditions? A compendium of religious truth whose authority and power rests in the simple assertion that it is the word of God? Or the living voice of God which springs to astonishing life when it is believed and obeyed in the power of the Holy Spirit?

What is Christian assurance? The blithe hope that all will be well? The quiet confidence that springs from believing the word of God whether its truth is felt or not? Or the leaping of the inner being in response to the promises of God, not only because they are objectively true but also because they have become subjectively real as the Spirit bears witness with our spirits that we are children of God?

What are the church's weapons in the great war? Good human organisation and shrewd methods? Dynamic personalities who can speak to millions? Memories of how the early church was supernaturally equipped, coupled with a confidence in the written Word? Or the full-orbed provision of gifts and graces, of offices and demonstrations, so that "the Gospel [comes] not only in word, but also in power and in the Holy Spirit and with full conviction" (1 Thessalonians 1:5)? A gospel which includes the 'public portraying of Christ crucified', the 'receiving of the Spirit', and 'the supply of the Spirit with the working of miracles' (see Galatians 3:1-5)?

What is Christian fellowship? The togetherness of people

with tastes in common? Membership of a local church which gives public allegiance to a set of divine truths and expresses them in worship once or twice a week? Or a deep level of mutual commitment that makes us ready to listen to one another, learn from one another, and trust one another with our fears and our follies? Is 'the blest tie that binds' strong enough to survive unwelcome rebuke, frank counsel, occasional mistakes, and demands on time, money and sympathy? Is it expressed, or even felt, at a level that leads to hard, practical sharing?

What is the basis of true Christian unity? How will Christ's prayer 'that they may all be one' (John 17:21) be visibly answered? Through episcopal ordination reaching back in unbroken succession to the apostles of Jesus themselves? Through fidelity to an episcopal, presbyterian or congregational organisation, or any permutation of all three, regulating every detail of the church's life and worship? Through sentimental attachment to the concept, 'all one in Christ Jesus', occasionally displayed in set-piece demonstrations? Or through mutual recognition of "all those who in every place call on the name of our Lord Jesus Christ, both their Lord and ours" (1 Corinthians 1:2)? Through joyful realisation that the Spirit blows where he wills, in the historic Catholic churches of east and west, in the mainline Protestant denominations, in the newer movements of Christian Brethren, Salvation Army, the Pentecostal churches, emerging groups throughout the world who worship a triune God uniquely revealed in the divine-human person of Jesus of Nazareth?

Now it would be absurd to suggest that only charismatic Christians give the right answers to these questions. But certainly charismatics underline the right answers with a new urgency and immediacy. And certainly those who draw back (and even ask charismatics to keep quiet and behave) must be very careful lest they seem in turn to be equivocating.

Karl Rahner, a prominent German Roman Catholic, has written, '[In the future] Christians . . . will be the little flock of the Gospel . . . And so they will feel themselves as brothers to one another. Practically all will have surrendered their hearts and lives to Jesus Christ by a personal and deliberate decision. There will be a few parasites for to be a Christian will offer no worldly advantage.

"The Church will be again a little flock of those sharing the same faith, the same hope, the same love. It will not pride itself on this, it will not think itself superior to earlier ages of the Church, but will obediently and thankfully accept its own age as is apportioned to it by the Lord and his Spirit."[2]

It is our view that only as the church is constantly renewed in the power of the Holy Spirit will it be able to face the future. We are deeply grateful to God for the personal renewal he has brought into our own lives, and for the corporate renewal he has brought into our churches. We pray he will continue his renewing work in the church and in the world, until "the kingdom of this world has become the kingdom of our God and of his Christ, and he shall reign for ever and ever" (Revelation 11:15)).

Notes
[1] See Dr James Dunn, *Baptism in the Holy Spirit* (SCM Press), 224ff.
[2] K. Rahner, *'The Christian of the Future'* in *Convergence 6* (1965), 3,4, quoted in Leon Joseph Cardinal Suenens, *A New Pentecost?* (Darton, Longman & Todd, 1976), 126, 127.

COLIN URQUHART

FAITH FOR THE FUTURE

The remarkable and inspiring sequel to When the Spirit Comes.

'God wants to give us all *faith for the future*, to believe that He will move among us in the coming years with greater power. He wants to give us His faith and teach us to see things as He sees them. He wants to bring us to the end of compromise in our lives and ministries. He calls all who belong to Him to be part of His building work as He fulfills His promise to build His Church.'

1981 is the year of the unexpected. The fellowship at The Hyde comes under new conviction of the holiness and glory of God. At the same time they realise anew that renewal is not enough: they can only bring revival to others if they are revived themselves. Later that year, they are told at the end of a mission in Wales, "This is how our parents described revival to us."

PETER ASAEL GONZALES

with Dan Wooding

PROPHETS OF REVOLUTION

The dramatic lives of one man and his family in the social and political upheavals of Latin America. Foreword by Brother Andrew.

Peter Gonzales, born and brought up in Mexico, took his first steps in the working world as a shoe-shine boy. His conversion to Christianity began a new adventure as he became convinced of the need for a spiritual revolution in Latin America.

He wasn't the only one concerned for change. Each of his brothers and sisters has become a 'prophet of revolution'. One is leading a literacy campaign in Nicaragua. Another is writing books about fighting injustice, and a third is organising co-operatives for artisans in Mexico. A burning Christian faith motivates this remarkable family. Peter himself has travelled all over Latin America for the United Bible Societies, more recently with Brother Andrew of Open Doors, and is now working full-time for Open Doors.

DONALD BRIDGE AND DAVID PHYPERS

THE MEAL THAT UNITES?

Bread and wine are at the heart of Christian worship. Their use is always special, but descriptions of this meal are bewilderingly varied. Some still withhold communion from those not in their own particular tradition.

Donald Bridge and David Phypers, a Baptist and an Anglican, provide a valuable introduction to the Eucharist of Lord's Supper. Biblical study, combined with the history of this Christian meal and an analysis of the present situation illuminate proposals for a way forward. Christians, they insist, must understand each others' views in the light of the Bible's teaching before all who break the one bread can really share it as one body.